To Aron and Jordan,
for the love you have brought into my life

CONTENTS

PREFACE

Human beings are embedded in a set of social relations. A social network is one way of conceiving that set of social relations in terms of a number of persons connected to one another by varying degrees of relatedness. In the early Jesus group documents featuring Paul and coworkers, it takes little effort to envision the apostle's collection of friends and friends of friends that is the Pauline network.

This set of brief books consists of a description of some of the significant persons who constituted the Pauline network. For Christians of the Western tradition, these persons are significant ancestors in faith. While each of them is worth knowing by themselves, it is largely because of their standing within that web of social relations woven about and around Paul that they are of lasting interest. Through this series we hope to come to know those persons in ways befitting their first-century Mediterranean culture.

Bruce J. Malina
Creighton University
Series Editor

ACKNOWLEDGMENTS

Numerous people have contributed to helping me complete this book. Bruce Malina asked me to contribute this volume when the series was first conceived. His patience in editing the material and raising valuable questions helped to clarify my thinking about many matters. The influence of my friends and colleagues in the Context Group can be seen throughout the work. During the period in which I was writing this book, the University of Pretoria and the William A. Freistat Center at Augustana College both provided generous funds that enabled me to attend an international meeting of the Context Group in Pretoria. Ernest van Eck was a delightful host and has shown me much friendship over the years. Both he and those in attendance at that conference, particularly John Kloppenborg, Zeba Crook, Pieter Botha, Pieter Craffert, and Alicia Batten, helped sharpen my thinking about a number of issues related to Peter. Zeba Crook also read most of the manuscript and contributed much useful critique. I truly appreciate his generosity with his time and his critical insight. My wife, Rikka, read the manuscript in progress several times and helped me understand when professional jargon made the work difficult to understand for someone who is not a biblical scholar. Her extraordinary grace and support exceed far beyond this type of help, and I am grateful for all of her support.

INTRODUCTION

The subject of this book is the New Testament personage known as "Peter." Perhaps what bears saying about him, first of all, is that his name was not really Peter at all. The name Peter is a nickname. The Greek name Peter is related to the Greek word for "rock," which means that Peter is a nickname much like the English name "Rocky." According to the Gospels of Mark, Luke, and John, he received this nickname from Jesus himself. Peter's original name is Simon, and it is by this name that he is known in the gospels before Jesus renames him Peter (Gk: *Petros*). Paul refers to Peter once as Peter (Gal 2:7-8) but, more commonly, by his Aramaic name, Kēphas (*Cephas* in most English translations of the New Testament).

This book is neither a life of Peter nor a critical biography of the historical Peter.[1] Its primary aim is not an examination of what details of Peter's life can be considered historical as opposed to those that are better attributed to legend. Neither is its purpose primarily literary, to examine the different ways in which Peter is presented in each of the gospels, though comparisons will be made between Peter as he is described by Paul and Peter as he is described in the gospels and in the book of Acts.[2] Such comparisons abound, but most of them do not address the difference between ancient and modern thinking about human personality. Nor do these modern descriptions of Peter really address what ancient Mediterranean people themselves deemed important in describing a person. This book examines Peter as an ancient Mediterranean person. In the early literary remains of the Jesus-movement groups, Peter is remembered as a proclaimer of the

1

kingdom of God, a change agent, an illiterate peasant fisherman, and a wonder-working orator in near-complete emulation of Jesus.

Peter was a person who lived in a very specific social and historical context. The context in which Peter lived was the first third of the first century CE in the territory of Galilee, near the eastern shore of the Mediterranean Sea. When Peter became part of the Jesus movement, Herod Antipas was ruling Galilee on behalf of the Romans as a tetrarch (a ruler of a "quarter portion") of the former kingdom of his father, Herod the Great. The area was largely occupied by Israelites, descendants of the patriarchs described in the Torah, the epic traditions of Israel contained in the first five books of the Hebrew Bible. This status as Israelites put the inhabitants of Galilee, together with the inhabitants of Judea, at odds with Roman political religion. The rulers of Rome developed propaganda that suggested it was the Roman gods who had established Rome's new golden age of rule over the entire inhabited world (Gk: *oikoumenē*). The Israelites, by contrast, honored the god of their ancestors, Yahweh. Yahweh had established a series of covenants with the Israelites, granting them, rather than the Romans, possession of the land they inhabited. For this reason, Roman rule, as had been the case when the Seleucids (an ancient Syrian dynasty) and the Ptolemies (an ancient Egyptian dynasty) ruled over them, caused the Israelites a number of difficulties. Not infrequently, loyalty to Israelite traditions was the cause of conflict with the Romans, notably manifesting itself in a series of armed conflicts with the Romans that ultimately led to the destruction of Jerusalem and its temple around 70 CE.

As one can clearly see, this cultural context is vastly different from the modern context of the United States. Tetrarchs are not part of modern North American government. Freedom of religion is part of modern, Western democracies, though religion is understood generally as a private, not a political, matter. This freedom, and the distinction between religion and politics, is part of a modern, Western notion of government based on the idea of individual rights and freedom. These ideals simply did not exist in first-century, circum-Mediterranean societies. In order to appreciate the culture in which Peter lived, it is important to bridge the cultural and historical gap between readers located in the modern United States and the writers of the texts found in the New Testament. Bridging this gap is no easy task. To understand the person of Peter, it is necessary to use appropriate lenses for understanding first-century, eastern Mediterranean societies. Helpfully, these lenses are provided by social scientists in the form of cultural-anthropological models.

A growing number of biblical scholars have been using approaches that adopt explicit use of cultural-anthropological models and theoretical principles from the social sciences for more than thirty years now.[3] These models can aid readers in understanding first-century Mediterranean persons like Peter. Models enable scholars, when studying groups from other cultural contexts, to be explicit about the assumptions they make.

The use of models allows scholars to avoid two pitfalls that oftentimes plague scholarship: anachronism and ethnocentrism. Anachronism is applying norms and values of modern times to documents from the past. Ethnocentrism is the application of one culture's values to another culture. When studying figures of the past who lived in significantly different cultural contexts, avoiding anachronism and ethnocentrism is both important and difficult. Most people, when they encounter other people, assume that the people they meet are like them in terms of their feelings, values, thoughts, and actions. People who make these assumptions when they travel to different cultural areas might soon find themselves experiencing "culture shock." Using anthropological models for understanding both our own cultures and those cultures about which we wish to learn enables us to recognize those places where different assumptions and patterns of socialization might result in our being insensitive readers of ancient texts. Use of these models provides a kind of interpretive key for understanding who Peter was and why he was significant for those authors who chose to write about him.

Ancient Personality:
Individualism and Collectivism

American culture, though it is not culturally monolithic, participates in a wider cultural stream labeled "Western" culture. To identify such a culture group is to indicate that Western cultures (by which scholars typically mean North American, though frequently excluding Mexico, and Western European countries) share some elements of perceiving the world. Western culture is marked by individualism:

> A preliminary definition of individualism is a social pattern that consists of loosely linked individuals who view themselves as independent of collectives; are primarily motivated by their own preferences, needs, rights, and the contracts they have established with others; give priority to their personal goals over the goals of others; and emphasize rational analyses of the advantages and disadvantages to associating with others.[4]

Individualism stresses two main things: the autonomy and rights of the individual person and the relative equality of all people. To be oneself means to make choices that are in the best interests of the individual. Peer pressure is considered a negative thing, and each individual is supposed to choose his or her own path in life. Americans are introspective, considering the important part of themselves to be hidden within the resources of their mind and psyche. To really know a modern American is to know what inner motivations make him or her do the things that he or she does. Individualists are socialized to feel guilt when they deviate from some culturally expected norm. It is almost inconceivable to most Americans that this way of thinking about people is relatively new in the history of thought. Without realizing it, many Americans transpose their individualist understandings of personhood onto other cultures that conceive of personhood much differently.

Ancient Mediterranean cultures were, by and large, collectivist. Harry Triandis defines collectivism as follows:

> Collectivism may be initially defined as a social pattern consisting of closely linked individuals who see themselves as parts of one or more collectives (family, co-workers, tribe, nation); are primarily motivated by the norms of, and duties imposed by, those collectives; are willing to give priority to the goals of these collectives over their personal goals; and emphasize their connectedness to members of the collectives.[5]

Collectivists operate with the best interests of the ingroup in mind. They subjugate their own personal interests to the desires of the group. Collectivists are shamed by those around them when they deviate from social norms. They are socialized to believe that the opinion of the group matters more than the individual's own consideration of her or his identity. For this reason, they are also socialized to think in stereotypes when considering members of various groups. In other words, people in a collectivistic culture tend to think that when they know where someone is from, or who their parents are, then they *know* that person.

The chart on page 6 shows some key differences between individualists and collectivists.[6]

Reading the Bible through the eyes of a Western individualist can cause modern people to read in culturally insensitive ways by importing ethnocentric and anachronistic concepts and questions to the biblical texts. Krister Stendahl, for example, has shown how modern Western people, using the idea of "introspective conscience," have asked questions of Paul's writings that they do not answer. Westerners have read Pauline texts as dealing with questions of doubt and inner motivations, a struggle with conscience in the individualist sense. Stendahl proposes, however, that these questions, while appropriate for modern Western persons, are not the questions that Paul was addressing in his letters. Paul's letters, rather, dealt with the

Individualists	Collectivists
People are encouraged to think of themselves and others as individuals and to avoid stereotypical thinking	People socialized to think of themselves as dyadic group members and to relate to others stereotypically
Individuals represent themselves alone and not the group of which they are a part	Individuals represent the groups of which they are a part
Individuals are expected to experience a great deal of social mobility and change	Individuals are expected to experience little or no social or geographical mobility
Individuals and groups are always changing; relationships come and go	Individuals and groups are predictable, stable, unchanging
Individually internalized norms (conscience) are main behavioral control	Socially supervised situations are main behavioral control
People freely join and leave communities; shallow rather than deep and long-term relationships	God (or fate, fortune, providence) controls social relationships
Relationships are based on equality; focus on peer-to-peer relationships	Social authority is from above; many key relationships are hierarchical
Reluctance to enter into private lives of others	Unwillingness to leave lives of others alone
Success is the outcome of free-market competition among individuals	Success is living up to and maintaining one's inherited social status
Individuals' true identity is found within themselves through introspection	Individuals and groups are endowed with clear and certain social identity
Individual is primary reality with society being a second-order, artificial, or derived construct	Society is the primary reality; individual is second-order construct
People think "individually" in terms of identity; who one is is largely dependent on that person	People think "socially" in group terms and employ inherited stereotypes

question of what to do about the law now that the Messiah had come. "Where Paul was concerned about the possibility for Gentiles to be included in the messianic community, his statements are now read as answers to the quest for assurance about man's [*sic*] salvation out of a common human predicament."[7] Western theologians and biblical scholars have assumed this common human problem to be one of guilt for the failure to keep the law. On the contrary, Paul did not seem to be plagued by such guilt when he describes his life either before or after his conversion. Paul's problem is how to establish a community rather than how to deal with his own troubled consciousness. Stendahl concludes "that the West for centuries has wrongly surmised that the biblical writers were grappling with problems which no doubt are ours, but which never entered their consciousness."[8]

Ancient persons were most concerned with knowing things that would be considered stereotypical by today's modern American standards. One's birthplace (geography), one's family line (generation), and one's gender were the most important things to know about a person in order to understand him or her in the first-century, eastern Mediterranean world,[9] largely because all people from a particular place or a particular family were considered to be in almost every meaningful way the same. This sameness was even the ideal for sons with respect to their fathers in Sirach: "When the father dies he will not seem to be dead, for he has left behind him one like himself" (Sir 30:4). Paul describes himself in terms of his descent on several occasions (Rom 11:1; 2 Cor 11:22; Phil 3:5). It is interesting that Paul himself does not tell his communities his place of origin. Acts, of course, fills in this information for him. Paul is from Tarsus (Acts 9:11; 21:39; 22:3). The author of Acts has Paul himself describe Tarsus as a not insignificant city (21:39).[10]

Almost all of these pieces of information about most of the important figures of Mediterranean antiquity are available to readers of ancient texts. What is perhaps most striking about Peter is that very little information is preserved regarding his generation. Apart from a mention of his father's name (Matt 16:17), there is little information regarding Peter's family.[11] Mark reports Peter's place of residence, his occupation, and his gender (Mark 1:16). There are other significant clues in the texts that give the sensitive reader information the ancient authors considered relevant. The effort will have to be made to understand how to "cognitively convert" the data considered into the appropriate setting to understand what the early readers/hearers of these texts would have read/heard in them.

Outline of the Book

The chapters of this book are dedicated to developing an understanding of Peter that would make sense to the people who wrote and heard the texts of the first generations of the Jesus movement. We must pay special attention, then, to the anthropological models that can help us understand the key items of the descriptions of Peter that we find in these texts. Chapter 1 of the book examines Peter's place in the Jesus tradition by discussing the interests of the first generations of the Jesus movement. Chapter 2 examines Peter as he is described in Paul's letters. In these letters, Peter is seen as a change agent, an honorable leading figure of the Jesus Messiah group at Jerusalem. Chapter 3 addresses the portraits of Peter found in the Synoptic Gospels, making use of the model of patronage and clientage and a description of the stratification of society in the Roman world to discuss Peter's role in proclaiming the forthcoming theocracy of the God of Israel. Chapter 4 addresses Peter as broker of the Spirit and moral entrepreneur in the book of Acts. Through experiences of altered states of consciousness, Peter is able to perform the same type of wonders as Jesus performs in the gospels. The letters attributed to Peter are assessed in chapter 5. Peter is remembered as a letter writer, addressing communities through a medium that was quite popular among followers of Jesus by the end of the first century CE.

CHAPTER 1

Peter's Place in the Jesus Tradition

According to the gospel accounts, Peter is a major figure among the group of Jesus' most intimate followers. When this group is given, Peter is always listed at the beginning, surely an indication of his place of prominence.[1] Peter belongs to the first generation of followers of Jesus. He was part of Jesus' social network, having been recruited to the movement by Jesus himself.

Generations of the Jesus Movement

To understand what it means that Peter belonged to the first generation of the Jesus movement, it is necessary to consider the characteristics of the generations of the Jesus movement. In an article detailing the Gospels of Mark, Matthew, and John as third-generation phenomena, Bruce Malina has described an account of the "generations" of the Jesus movement.[2] Malina, building on the work of sociologist Marcus Hansen,[3] explains that "when a first generation has experienced significant and irreversible change the second generation seeks to ignore (hence 'forget') many dimensions of first generation experience, while the third generation seeks to remember and recover what the second generation sought to forget."[4] A generation is not necessarily only a chronological designation in this theory:

> While the term has a temporal, chronological dimension, its main feature is sequential, a single step in a line of descent. The category can be applied to generations of those affiliated with Jesus. Those Jesus group members who assisted Jesus, witnessed his activity and regrouped after his crucifixion and his initial appearances belonged to the first step in the line of descent from Jesus. . . . This first generation included Jesus, his core group members, their family members along with friends and followers who belonged to their social network.[5]

Even today the term "generation" does not indicate only chronology. First, in modern North America, life expectancy is considerably longer than it was in first-century Galilee. For this reason, most families have three or four generations living at a time. Even in antiquity, however, generations overlapped one another to some extent. Second, "generation" is a bit of a slippery term. I am part of Generation X, but it is not clear exactly what birth years designate the beginning and end of this generation. Generations are frequently defined by things like worldview, outlook, sociological trends, and chronology. In the same way, the generations of the Jesus movement are designated to some extent by their relationship to Jesus and by ideologies concerning him and his movement.

Malina notes that this first generation was concerned with "proclaiming a forthcoming Israelite theocracy."[6] A theocracy is direct rule by God. This generation understood Jesus as a prophet who announced the impending arrival of this theocracy, who recruited followers to aid him in spreading the message, and who insisted on repentance in order to get "their affairs in order and aligned with God's will."[7] Preparation for the forthcoming theocracy included performing healings and exorcisms and living in accordance with Jesus' countercultural teachings.

"Initially, what Jesus' faction members were to do was assist Jesus in proclaiming the gospel of the kingdom and healing and exorcism with a view to the kingdom."[8] This first generation experienced a significant change that was irreversible in Jesus' crucifixion and subsequent appearances.

Jesus' death and resurrection changed the focus of the proclamation of the first generation. Though they still proclaimed the kingdom of God after Jesus' death and the resurrection appearances, they shifted the focus of the proclamation to Jesus as Israel's Messiah.[9] This group was the reconstituted group of Jesus' faction members after the resurrection appearances. They proclaimed that God would soon take control of Israel through his anointed agent, the Messiah Jesus. Their primary mission was to let all of Israel know that Jesus, by virtue of God having raised him, was the Messiah and that they should prepare for his return with power.

The drastic change of Jesus' death and resurrection led to a reconfiguration of the thinking regarding the forthcoming theocracy, but it also entailed the rise of new key players. "Paul and his contemporaries, in turn, marked a second step in the line of descent of this fictive kin group, a second generation."[10] The second generation chose to "forget" elements of concern to the first generation.[11] This forgetting is the main reason that Paul's letters do not contain many teachings of Jesus. Rather than focusing on the activities and teachings of Jesus, this second generation focused on what God had done to Jesus in his death and resurrection. The second generation understood Jesus primarily as a cosmic agent existing with God in the heavenly realm, not as a teacher/healer brokering God's rule. This new way of understanding Jesus, as a heavenly agent, led to several key shifts in thinking about Jesus. Jesus came to be considered as a being different from an ordinary human. Some members of the second generation abandoned the observation of some Judean customs and increasingly focused on all Israel rather than a small faction of those loyal to Jesus' vision of God's forthcoming rule.[12]

Second-generation Jesus groups were criticized both by first-generation Jesus groups and by Israelites who were not followers of Jesus. The first-generation Jesus groups accused them of "displacing the role of Torah in favor of primacy of the Spirit of Jesus" and criticized "their focus on Jesus, not theocracy" and "their lack of interest in what exactly Jesus said and did."[13] In other words, they focused on access to Jesus as a heavenly figure rather than as a teacher and failed to proclaim the kingdom of God in the same way that the first-generation disciples had. Israelites who were not followers of Jesus accused them of apostasy because of their lack of concern for traditional Israelite practices such as eating only clean foods. They were also criticized for their focus on "Jesus as Israel's Messiah soon to come," which might have resulted in unwanted attention from the Romans, and for their implied rejection of the current arrangement of Israel by focusing on a forthcoming shift to theocracy mediated by Christ as cosmic Lord.[14]

The third generation remembered things from the first generation that the second generation forgot. These things included many items recollected from the first generation. These "remembrances," however, are not identical to the things that the first generation taught. According to Marcus Lee Hansen, third-generation groups recall things important to the experience of the first generation, but the third generation casts these memories into categories and narratives that speak to their own experience.[15] So, rather than repeating what the first generation said, the third generation recasts important tenets of first-generation thinking and recontextualizes these thoughts into new frameworks for understanding the world. In this way, they reproduce the past by claiming what is significant about it while minimizing other elements that are not significant to the later generation.[16]

In terms of the Jesus tradition, third-generation documents include the Synoptic Gospels. It is in these texts that early Jesus movements refocus on the words of Jesus, even as they "produce" words of Jesus and introduce new contexts in which to understand these words. The narrative gospels demonstrate precisely how such changes can occur. The renewed focus on the kingdom of God is melded with the focus of second-generation Jesus groups concerned with Jesus' role as cosmic agent. The image of the kingdom of God is no longer only for members of the house of Israel but is available to all who would faithfully follow Jesus.

The following chart helps to distinguish the significant elements of the first three generations of the Jesus movement.[17]

First generation	Second generation	Third generation
Members included Jesus and his core group members, their families, and others in their social network	Interested in the universality of God's action in raising Jesus	Interested in what was lost by the second-generation Jesus groups
The original Galilean faction engaged in proclaiming the forthcoming Israelite theocracy and preparing people for the event through healing and exorcism	Proclaimed Jesus as resurrected Lord at God's right hand; understood Jesus as a heavenly being	Interested in the kingdom of God due to interest in the past rather than an expectation of its forthcoming arrival
Interested in what Jesus taught and did	Lack of interest in what Jesus taught and did	Renewed interest in the teachings of Jesus
Characterized by countercultural wisdom	Understood Jesus as resurrected Lord; developed "incipient" Christology	Developed the "biography" of Jesus in order to describe the full story of Jesus
Focus on Israel/Israelites to the exclusion of Gentiles	How to include various ethnic groups (Gk: *ethnē*) is a key question	Maintain an interest in the inclusion of *ethnē*
Main group is the faction that Jesus recruits to live God's rule/kingdom	Interested in what God had done to Jesus in raising him and the forthcoming kingdom of God	Documents of the third generation are reappropriations of first-generation events and stories that are made applicable to third generation interest
Largely Aramaic-speaking, not Greek	Largely Greek-speaking	Largely Greek-speaking, though with some reference to Aramaic

Our sources tell us that Peter was a part of the first generation of the Jesus movement. He was one of Jesus' most intimate followers. Recruited in Galilee, he proclaimed the kingdom of God (forthcoming theocracy) to Israelites, some of whom he also healed or from whom he cast out unclean spirits. This generation experienced a drastic change because of Jesus' crucifixion. After his death and the resurrection appearances, these members of the first generation shifted from being a "Jesus group" to being a "Jesus Messiah group." This shift involved proclaiming Jesus as Israel's Messiah who was soon to return as judge. No account written by first-generation followers of Jesus still exists. Jesus and his disciples left no written materials. Paul's letters are the earliest sources we have about Peter, and those sources are part of the second-generation Jesus movement. The gospels postdate these letters by as many as two to four decades. The gospels are third-generation Jesus-group materials. Much of the information typically used to reconstruct the "historical" Peter, in fact, comes from a fourth-generation source, the book of Acts.

The information about Peter passed along by the second-, third-, and fourth-generation Jesus groups omits much information that modern biographers deem important. Peter's age at the time of his call by Jesus is unknown, and we know nothing of his birth or death from the New Testament. There is conflicting information about Peter's hometown. Though several sources indicate that Peter was married, information regarding his wife is absent from these texts. Paul indicates in 1 Corinthians that Peter was supported by local communities of Jesus groups during at least some points of his lifetime. It is clear that no one in the earliest generations of the Jesus movement set out to write a life of Peter. In Acts, the New Testament document in which Peter plays the most prominent role, he eventually fades from the scene with no account of his ultimate destiny.

The model of generations of the early Jesus movement can help clarify several major points about the portrayals of Peter that are preserved in the writings of the New Testament. With only a couple of exceptions, Peter does not feature prominently in the literature of the second generation of Jesus followers. Indeed, the only occasions in which Peter is discussed in the literature of the second generation (Galatians and 1 Corinthians) involve events at Jerusalem, the question of how to include non-Judeans into the Jesus movement, or factions within recently founded Jesus groups. In the third generation of the Jesus movement, however, Peter again becomes a major figure. His relationship to Jesus is remembered by those who write the "biographies" of Jesus. In the fourth-generation work Acts, Peter is described as being in total harmony with the other leaders of a unified Jesus movement that begins in Jerusalem and moves from there toward Rome, the imperial city.

CHAPTER 2

Peter in the Second Generation of the Jesus Movement

Every person has a social network.[1] One's social network consists of all the people whom one knows personally but also some people with whom one is not personally acquainted. Social networks consist of several zones. The first-order zone includes those people with whom one has direct contact. Jeremy Boissevain calls them "friends." The second-order zone refers to friends of friends. The third-order zone includes friends of friends of friends. In social-network theory, interaction is the key criterion for understanding how groups and societies are formed and maintained. "A person's network thus forms a social environment from and through which pressure is exerted to influence his [sic] behaviour; but it is also an environment through which he [sic] can exert pressure to affect the behaviour of others."[2] The social network, then, is the means by which a person can influence those around him or her to cause people to do what he or she wants them to do. Such influence, of course, does not go only one way. As friends of a person might be influenced by her, so those same friends might also influence her.

We can use two first-year college students, Jack and Jill, as examples. If these two students do not know one another and if they do not have mutual friends, they are not part of one another's social networks. If, however, Jack meets Jill's friend from back home, then he is now a friend of a friend of Jill's and properly belongs to Jill's social network, even if they still have not met. He is part of Jill's second-order zone. If Jack and Jill met in a class, they would become part of each other's first-order zones.

Now, while they may be first-order friends, since they know each other directly, it is still a simple relationship. They share only one role in common: they are fellow students in a class. At this stage, if Jill wanted to borrow Jack's car, it is unlikely that Jack would agree to such a thing. Were they to become study partners, however, they would have a second role that coincided. If Jill began dating Jack's roommate, the relationship between Jack and Jill would have a third connection. At this point, Jack might be more willing to lend his car to Jill. There is a high likelihood that Jack and Jill would see each other more frequently than if they shared a single role. If the relationship between Jack and his roommate was friendly, Jack and Jill might even invest more time and energy to get to know one another and become close friends. It is possible, however, that if Jill and Jack's roommate were to break up, then Jack and Jill would go out of their way to avoid one another.

Each of the elements of the relationship between Jack and Jill is related to four interactional criteria that are useful for network analysis. The interactional criteria are (1) diversity of linkages, (2) transactional content, (3) directional flow, and (4) frequency and duration of interaction.

Diversity of linkages is also termed "multiplexity" by Boissevain. Multiplexity refers to the number of ways in which people are connected to one another. "A social relation between two people that is based on a single role relation is described as uniplex or single-stranded, while a relation that covers many roles is termed multiplex or many-stranded."[3] If people are connected by a single role, the relationship is less likely to be deep.

In uniplex relationships, "friends" are less likely to influence each other in very many ways. Multiplex relations, those in which friends have several overlapping roles in common, tend to provide greater accessibility and typically are more intimate than uniplex relations. When Jack and Jill have only a single class together, we would expect a rather shallow relationship. As Jack and Jill have more roles that overlap, the relationship between them would be deeper, and they would be more likely to influence each other's behavior.

Transactional content refers to "the material and non-material elements which are exchanged by two actors in a particular role relation or situation."[4] When people exchange things (importantly including non-material items) that they consider highly significant, each will invest more in the relationship, and each will anticipate a greater benefit from the relationship. Transactional content is exchanged between Jack and Jill both when they are study partners (in the form of information and study habits) and when Jack lends his car to Jill. Multiplex relationships usually involve the transaction of more (and more significant) content.

Directional flow refers "to the direction in which the elements exchanged move."[5] When items exchanged are equal or become equal over time, it is an indication that the parties are equal in status, but when "there is asymmetry . . . there is very often a difference in status and power between the actors."[6] In modern North American societies, most relationships are ideally relationships among equals. Directional flow in most relationships, then, is expected to be equal. Modern North Americans generally consider relationships in which one person is indebted consistently to another person to be problematic. In first-century Mediterranean societies, however, such indebtedness was a common practice. In the example of Jack and Jill, while they are study partners, both are expected to bring some information or knowledge to the partnership. If one member of a study group does not contribute, close relationships are not likely to develop between that person and others in the group. The relationship is supposed to be mutually beneficial.

Finally, frequency and duration of interaction indicate how much time people are willing to invest in relationships with others. More frequent and longer-lasting contact is typically indicative of the value that the actors place upon the relationship. In modern North American social networks, people come and go with sometimes amazing frequency. This fact is due in large part to our geographic mobility. When we move, relationships can go from being multiplex to uniplex, and the intensity of such relationships changes. In first-century Mediterranean societies, geographic mobility was far less common for the vast majority of the population, so relationships typically remained multiplex and intense. In our example above, Jack and Jill might be close while they are in college, especially if they see each other on a daily basis, but they may not remain close if their careers take them to different parts of the country and they no longer see one another regularly. Whether they take the time to maintain the relationship is dependent on their other time commitments and how much they value the relationship.

Paul's Encounters with Peter

These same observations about friendship and networks can be applied to Peter and Paul. Peter and Paul were part of each other's social networks due to the fact that they met one another, but we have very little information about their encounters. In fact, Paul mentions Peter in only two of his writings, Galatians and 1 Corinthians.

Only in Galatians does Paul indicate that the two ever met or spent any time together.[7] In Galatians, moreover, their situation seems to go from friendly to hostile. Paul narrates three separate encounters with Peter, or *Kēphas* as Paul calls him most often: three years after Paul's vision of the risen Christ (Gal 1:18-19), a second encounter fourteen years after the first (Gal 2:1-10), and a third (final?) encounter in Antioch some time after the second meeting in Jerusalem (Gal 2:11-14). In this last encounter, Peter and Paul are at odds with one another. The disagreement between them involves who should be a part of the Jesus movement and under what circumstances. Peter withdraws from eating with non-Judean (Gk: *ethnē*) members of the Jesus group in Antioch. Paul opposes Peter's withdrawal and wishes to expand the Jesus movement to include those who do not practice Judean customs (i.e., by eating "clean" foods with "clean" people). This type of disagreement, as we shall see below, is precisely the type that we might expect between first- and second-generation Jesus-group members.

The first generation consists of those who were part of Jesus' network during his lifetime, focused on the forthcoming reign of God. Peter is part of the first generation and is interested in Jesus' message of the immediately forthcoming rule of God among those who are faithful to God. For Peter, faithfulness to God entails an acceptance of basic *halakhic* practices (those practices based on Israelite laws and their interpretations) on which Paul does not insist for the non-Judean followers of Jesus. Peter is interested in how Jesus is relevant to his understanding of the renewed Israel in covenant with God.

On the other hand, Paul, as a second-generation member of the Jesus movement, is not interested in requiring non-Judean followers of Jesus to observe these *halakhic* practices. Rather, he is interested in understanding Jesus as a cosmic, and therefore universal, figure. For Paul, life in the spirit of Christ is the most important thing and takes precedence over the teachings of the historical Jesus.[8] This second generation, focused on "the significance of Jesus' being raised from the dead by the God of Israel, views Jesus as more than Israel's Messiah; the Resurrected Jesus was seated on God's right hand, was Lord."[9]

Paul's description of Peter in 1 Corinthians also makes sense in this context. In 1 Corinthians 15:5, Paul reports that the risen Christ "appeared to [Kēphas], then to the twelve." For Paul, such an appearance authorized Peter as an apostle (1 Cor 9:5). This appearance to Peter is not distinguished in kind (only in chronology) from the appearance of the risen Christ to Paul (1 Cor

15:8). What it does not do, however, is legitimate a coalition in Corinth that claimed Peter as its leader (1 Cor 1:12; 3:22).

There is much about the relationship between Peter and Paul that is lost to modern research. Their relationship appears to be uniplex. The one role that binds them (according to Paul's account) is that they are both apostles in the Jesus movement. Given the infrequency with which they see each other (Paul insists only three times in more than fourteen years), it is likely that the relationship was not very deep and that there was limited transactional content. In fact, Paul goes out of his way to say that Kēphas and James added nothing to his gospel (Gal 2:6). Despite Paul's protestations, the directional flow of the relationship seems to indicate that Kēphas was the higher status party. From Paul's account, the relationship between them seems to end with the confrontation described in Galatians 2:11-14. It is clear that, though they belong to the same social network, the transactions between these two figures are quite limited.

Peter in 1 Corinthians

Peter is mentioned four times in 1 Corinthians. The first two times he is mentioned (1:12 and 3:22) make it clear that there were some members of the Corinthian Jesus group(s) who were part of a coalition that claimed Peter as their leader. In Paul's description of the Jesus group(s) at Corinth, he discusses information he has received from "Chloe's people" (1:11) about coalitions within the group there. Paul says that certain members of the Jesus group there are claiming to belong to Paul, Apollos, Kēphas, or Christ (1:12). Paul appeals to the unity of the group in Christ and rejects the importance of the coalitions that have formed claiming allegiance to these "human leaders" (3:21). For Paul, then, Kēphas is among those who belong to the Corinthians "to Christ" (3:22-23). These texts tell us very little about Peter specifically. Peter is invoked by some members of the Corinthian community as a leader for a particular coalition. It is not clear from the text whether Peter had ever gone to Corinth, and there is no evidence elsewhere in the New Testament to suggest that he did. It is due to the fact that Peter is known as an apostle that these members of the Corinthian Jesus group can appeal to his authority.

These people who appeal to Peter's authority are part of his social network. They are probably not part of Peter's first-order zone. They are more likely people who had been recruited to the Jesus movement by friends of Peter or friends of friends of Peter. Peter's authority is invoked perhaps because he is known as an apostle (1 Cor 9:5; 15:5). For Paul, the chief characteristic that designates a person an "apostle" is seeing the resurrected Jesus (1 Cor 9:1).[10] In the list of those to whom the resurrected Jesus appears, Paul includes Kēphas in the first place and ends the list with himself (1 Cor 15:5-11). For Paul, one of the problems with the Jesus group in Corinth is that the friends of friends of Peter are influencing the behavior of the friends of Paul there. Paul's known acquaintances, Chloe and her people, are being negatively affected by the actions of those claiming allegiance to Peter. From Paul's perspective, those claiming allegiance to Peter are introducing an innovation into the Corinthian Jesus group (1 Cor 1:12). Paul does not consider the people introducing this innovation to be authorized change agents, though he does acknowledge Peter as such.

Change agents fulfill the social role of communicating innovation.[11] If successful, a change agent can persuade a client or audience to adopt an innovation. Such innovations can be new ideas, new technologies, or new practices. A change agent communicates the innovation desired by a change agency to an audience. Because the change agent represents the interests of one party (the change agency) to another party (the clients or audience), the change agent has a foot in two worlds. The change agent is usually one who has accepted the innovation for him- or herself or sees the value in doing so. Frequently, the change agent has a higher degree of specialization regarding the innovation than do the members of the audience to whom he or she communicates. The change agent may also have higher levels of education or a higher social or economic status. These differences between the change agent and the audience to whom he or she is communicating can create a situation in which the change agent is not trusted by those whom he or she wishes to persuade to adopt the innovation. More successful change agents are frequently those who are most like or most empathetic toward their clients.

Apostles were one type of change agent in the early Jesus movement. Apostles, however, were not the only kind of change agents operating in the Jesus movement. Paul knows of several other kinds (i.e., prophets, teachers, wonder workers, healers), though he ranks apostles as the highest of all the change agents (1 Cor 12:28). To be an apostle is to be sent on behalf of a superior agent (i.e., a change agency) to carry or proclaim a message. Peter fulfills this role since he was commissioned by God, who revealed the risen Jesus to both Peter and Paul. An apostle is a person who bears a message. In the case of these apostles, the message is from the God of Israel and is a message of innovation. In this way, apostles are change agents. They proclaim a message that is different from that of the traditional Israelite prophets because they proclaim that God had raised Jesus from the dead.

According to Paul, as an apostle, Peter was commissioned by a change agency (in this case, the God of Israel) by virtue of the appearance of the risen Jesus to him. The innovation that he proclaimed was that Jesus was the Messiah of Israel who would return soon with power to inaugurate God's kingdom. Peter was a person who had adopted the innovation he proclaimed. Since he had seen the risen Jesus, he had a more specialized knowledge and experience regarding the innovation he proclaimed. Those in Corinth who proclaimed their loyalty to Peter were adopters of Peter's message of innovation. It is unlikely, though, that Peter himself ever went to Corinth to proclaim the innovation that the God of Israel had given to him. Friends of Peter or friends of friends of Peter had introduced his innovation in Corinth, and some of the Corinthian Jesus-group members now spread the message of innovation on his behalf there. The Corinthians who claimed Peter as the head of their coalition likely did not know Peter directly. They were friends of friends of Peter or perhaps friends of friends of friends. They were not part of Peter's first-order zone in his network but were second- or third-order-zone members of his network.

Peter in Galatians

Peter and Paul met on three separate occasions (Gal 1:18-20; 2:1-10; 2:11-14). During the first of these encounters, Peter, or Kēphas as Paul calls him here, hosts Paul for fifteen days. We do not know how Paul and Peter first came to know one another. It is unclear whether someone introduced the two or whether someone had written a letter of recommendation to Peter on Paul's behalf. They were likely friends of friends, having common friends in some Jesus group at that time. What we do know is that Kēphas is one of two leaders with whom Paul met at Jerusalem. The other was James, "the Lord's brother" (Gal 1:19). This meeting makes Paul friends of both Kēphas and James, though friendship in the first-century Mediterranean context did not necessarily imply either equality or warmth of feeling as it does in modern North American contexts.[12] Paul says that, beyond these two, he did not meet with any other apostles in Jerusalem. The purpose of Paul's visit with Kēphas is not described. Paul, given his insistence that he did not learn his gospel from any human source, probably did not go to Kēphas to get his story straight concerning the gospel.

First-century Judean culture was an honor-shame culture. Honor can be defined as "the status one claimed in the community, together with the all-important public recognition of that claim."[13] In a collectivist culture in which people are socialized as members of groups, such public recognition by one's group is an important part of one's identity. Where a claim to honor is made but not upheld by the public, the person who makes such a claim is shamed. Peter is an honorable figure in the Jerusalem community because he is known as an apostle (Gal 1:18-19). His claim to status is recognized by the members of the Jerusalem Jesus community.

Paul made a second visit to Jerusalem fourteen years after the first (Gal 2:1). He acknowledges that Kēphas, James, and John were honored as leaders of the Jesus Messiah groups (Gal 2:2), though Paul himself seems to reject their claims to honor (Gal 2:6: "what they actually were makes no difference to me; God shows no partiality"). During the course of this meeting (narrated in Gal 2:1-10), a meeting between the "acknowledged leaders" (Gal 2:2) and Paul—together with his companions Barnabas and Titus—took place. The controversy surrounded the gospel that Paul preached to the "peoples" (Gk: *ethnē*; Gal 2:2). Paul laid his gospel before the acknowledged leaders. The outcome of the meeting was a division between Kēphas's mission and Paul's mission. Kēphas was to proclaim the gospel among the circumcised, while Paul was to proclaim it among the uncircumcised (Gal 2:7). Interestingly, Galatians 2:7-8 is the only place in Paul's letters where he refers to Kēphas as "Peter." These leaders gave to Paul and Barnabas "the right hand of fellowship" (Gal 2:9). This extension of the right hand might signify any number of things, though here it seems to indicate "a way of establishing an agreement, friendship or good faith."[14] Such agreements could imply "an inviolable pledge of protection, support or safe-conduct."[15] This gesture, undertaken publicly, would bind the parties to the agreement stated in Galatians 2:7-8. According to Paul, the apostles at Jerusalem, recognized leaders of the Jesus Messiah groups, did not add to Paul's gospel (Gal 2:6) but instead offered a public acknowledgment that he had received such a revelation. They granted Paul's status claim as an apostle. Alternatively, they could have shamed him by denying his claim to status. In any case, we can say from Paul's first and second visits with Kēphas in Jerusalem that Kēphas was known by others as an apostle, a change agent on behalf of the God of Israel.

The agreement, however, was not upheld, as is made clear in Galatians 2:11-14. The reason for this is already alluded to in Galatians 2:4. There, Paul says that "false believers" (the Greek term here, *adelphoi*, is properly understood as "siblings") entered the meeting to "spy on" the event so as to "enslave" Paul and his companions (and presumably also those who adopted Paul's innovation). This infiltration of the meeting by these false siblings made the meeting a "public" event rather than a private meeting (with only the acknowledged leaders).

The third encounter between Peter and Paul involves those false siblings (or people who represented their interests) arriving in Antioch. Peter had traveled to Antioch, though Paul does not say when or why he did so. During the time Peter spent in Antioch, he changed his behavior from eating with the *ethnē* to withdrawing from table fellowship with them. This change of behavior took place, from Paul's perspective, due to Peter's "fear" of the "circumcision faction" (Gal 2:12). This party was a group that insisted on circumcision for those men who ate together as members of the Jesus group in Antioch. Paul tells us that "until certain people came from James" (Gal 2:12), Kēphas ate with the *ethnē*. Once these people arrived, he withdrew from table fellowship with the *ethnē*. For this reason, Paul "opposed him to his face" (Gal 2:11). Having previously agreed (by offering the right hand of fellowship to Paul and Barnabas) to support Paul's proclamation to the uncircumcised, Kēphas now withdrew from the public support he had previously given. James's friends exercised an influence over Peter's behavior that caused him to withdraw from his previous behavior (Gal 2:12).

Kēphas's behavior influenced Paul's friends at Antioch. Paul himself is concerned, especially since the rest of the Judeans there, even Barnabas, a mutual "friend" of Peter and Paul, had followed Peter's behavior in withdrawing from eating with the *ethnē* (Gal 2:13). The change in the behavior of Kēphas was due to the arrival of men from James. These men were, at the least, friends of friends of Kēphas since Kēphas and James were known personally to one another. Paul's critique of Kēphas's behavior has to do with the influence that Kēphas had on those in Paul's social network. That Paul mentions Barnabas by name indicates that Paul considered his relationship to Barnabas a deeper relationship than that between Kēphas and Barnabas. Social networks, as discussed above, are the primary ways in which people influence the behavior of others. In the case of the Antioch incident, Paul's difficulty seems to be that Kēphas influenced Paul's friends after Paul thought that they agreed he would not do so (Gal 2:7). James, Barnabas, Kēphas, and Paul are all friends in network terms, though the influence they have over one another varies considerably from one context to the next.

The differences between Kēphas and Paul in Antioch can be accounted for by considering the differences between the first generation and the second, and a division within the second generation. As a member of the first generation of the Jesus movement (the Jesus Messiah group), Peter thought it obligatory to maintain the *halakhic* practices such as circumcision and the eating of clean food with clean people, at least after "certain people . . . from James" arrived in Antioch (Gal 2:12). Even though Paul and Peter were both change agents proclaiming an innovation from the God of Israel to various clients, they did not proclaim the change in the same way. Due to their being from different generations of the Jesus movement, Paul and Peter understood the meaning of Jesus' resurrection in quite different ways. We have seen that Peter was a member of a Jesus Messiah group. These groups proclaimed the forthcoming theocracy, emphasizing Jesus' role as Messiah and the expectation of his imminent return with power. Paul, on the other hand, belonged to the second generation of the Jesus movement. As we saw above, the interests of the second-generation Jesus-group members differed from those of the first generation.

One of the key differences between the first- and second-generation Jesus groups was the shift from organization as a political action group (with a focus on the rule of God as a patron) to a focus on a fictive kinship association. The first generation of the Jesus movement participated in the political religion of Jesus, while the second generation focused instead on treating one another like kin-group members should, though they were not themselves kin-group members. They organized themselves, however, along the pattern of a family and household.[16] In these groups, the "change sought is intergroup."[17]

The members of the Jesus groups at Antioch were members of the second generation of the Jesus group. Within the second generation, however, a split occurred. The second generation was divided into two sometimes competing groups: Messianic Jesus groups and Resurrected Jesus groups.[18] The non-Judean members of the Antioch Jesus group belonged to the Resurrected Jesus groups, while the interests of Messianic Jesus groups were represented as well. The Messianic Jesus groups insisted that Judean customs be observed regarding what type of food may be consumed and with whom, while the second group (in this case including Paul) insisted otherwise. Messianic Jesus groups "would insist on the rules of no mixing with the Gentiles. In effect, non-Israelite males who wished to join the group would have to become circumcised and follow Israel's kosher rules as they were among 'the circumcised.'"[19] These groups were fictive kinship associations for whom faithfulness to the Torah of Israel was of paramount importance. The second type of group in the second generation was Resurrected Jesus groups.

> In the ideology of these groups, the resurrected Jesus was a new revelation of God to Israel. Jesus was cosmic lord, cosmic broker or mediator before the God of Israel, and called by God for all. And since God's call might now be directed to all persons in the empire, God could now be conceived as the God of the *oikoumene*, a truly monotheistic God.[20]

These groups were less interested in the maintenance of *halakhic* practices on the part of non-Judean members of the Jesus movement. Circumcision was not a requirement for entrance to the movement for Resurrected Jesus groups. The difference between these two groups of second-generation followers is on display in the problems that developed in Antioch that Paul describes in the first two chapters of the letter to the Galatians. The agreement between Peter and Paul in Galatians 2:7-8 had to do with where their respective messages would be proclaimed. Peter would proclaim his message among the circumcised (who were located predominantly in Judea and its immediate environs), while Paul would proclaim his message among the uncircumcised (those more distant from Judea). Antioch, situated as it was in Syria (north of Galilee), was a site populated by both circumcised and uncircumcised. In this location, the tensions between the first-generation Jesus Messiah groups, with support from the second-generation Messianic Jesus groups, came into tension with the second-generation Resurrected Jesus groups.

Conclusion

In the second generation, we can see that Peter was known as an apostle, a change agent designated by the God of Israel to proclaim the gospel due to the fact that the risen Jesus had appeared to him. In Corinth, he was claimed as a leader of a coalition, despite the fact that he never went there. In Galatians, Peter is a leader of the Jesus Messiah group at Jerusalem. He is a first-generation member of the Jesus group who practices the political religion of Jesus, proclaiming him as the Messiah soon to return to inaugurate the kingdom of God. His adherence to the practices and beliefs of the first-generation Jesus group cause a problem for Paul when his adherence to Judean custom brings him into conflict with the change agent of the second-generation Resurrected Jesus group, Paul.

CHAPTER 3

Peter in the Synoptic Gospels

The Gospels of Mark and Matthew come from the third generation of the Jesus movement. Luke, together with its companion volume Acts, comes from the fourth generation of the Jesus movement. As we would expect from third-generation documents, these gospels tell the story of Jesus, the person who lived in first-century Galilee.[1] They tell this story, however, from the vantage point of the third generation. They are interested in Jesus and his disciples not only because they are interested in the past but also because the authors of the gospels appropriate the stories about Jesus and his disciples for the interests of the third generation. Paul's letters demonstrate very little concern for the life of Jesus apart from isolated elements of the final week of Jesus' life and a major focus on his death and resurrection. The third generation rediscovers the narrative about Jesus. The words and deeds of Jesus, however, are read through the experiences of third-generation members of the Jesus movement. "As third-generation remembrance, Jesus stories were appropriated and elaborated, told with a view to relevance in new situations, recontextualized after a fashion."[2] Ingroup and outgroup boundaries are drawn in different ways so as to include those who live according to the reign of God.[3] Though looking back to a time when the Jesus movement was a Jesus Messiah group, the third generation was not organized around Israelite political religion. They were a fictive kinship association.

An Aside on the Q Source

The first three New Testament gospels tell remarkably similar stories of Jesus. These three gospels are often referred to as "Synoptic" because they "see together" (Gk: *sunopsis*) the story of Jesus. The narrative outline of these three gospels is very similar, especially when one compares them to the Gospel of John or to any of the preserved gospels that were not included in the New Testament. Due to this similarity, most scholars believe that one of the three Synoptic Gospels was used as a source by the other two. Figuring out which one came first and what the others copied from the earliest one is called the "Synoptic Problem."[4] The vast majority of modern biblical scholars think that Mark is the earliest of the Synoptic Gospels and that Mark is a basic source for Matthew and Luke. Even after identifying Mark as a source for the other two Synoptic Gospels, Matthew and Luke have a great deal of material in common that is not found in Mark's gospel. This material, consisting mostly of teachings of Jesus, comes from a source called "Q." Q is the designation given to this text because it is an abbreviation for the German word *Quelle* ("source"). Since there is no longer an ancient copy of this source, scholars have to reconstruct the source based on the comparison of the common sayings traditions found in Matthew and Luke.[5] The reconstructed text of Q consists almost entirely of sayings of Jesus because these sayings are the main material that Matthew and Luke share that is not found in Mark.

There is no mention of Peter (or any other named disciple) in Q. James Robinson suggests one possible reason why the disciples are not named in the document. He says that "the disciples of the Q movement do not seem to have been these leaders stationed in Jerusalem" (i.e., James, Kēphas/Peter, John).[6] Robinson goes further to note that the "'apostles' and the 'twelve' are not mentioned in Q, either by title or by name."[7]

There is another possible reason, however, why Peter and the other disciples are not named in Q. According to Robinson, Q is the "earliest witness" to Jesus. Q represents the interests of the "first generation" of Jesus' disciples.[8] The focus of Q rests squarely on the notion of the reign/rule/kingdom of God, the very thing that most historical Jesus scholars link with Jesus himself.[9] The first generation "engaged in assisting Jesus in proclaiming a forthcoming Israelite theocracy and in preparing Israelites for the event through healing and exorcism."[10] Given that this generation focused more on the message of Jesus than on the person of Jesus, such a lack of focus on individual named disciples might not surprise readers. The disciples, as they are described in Q 10:5-9,[11] participate in announcing the reign/kingdom of God and in healing and exorcism. The disciples are coworkers in the preparation for the forthcoming Israelite theocracy. To the first generation, engaged in the performance of Jesus' movement, the identity of the participants is not yet a matter of reflection. For this reason, it is not surprising that the Q source would provide no information about Peter.

Remembering Jesus: Social Memory and the Third-Generation Jesus Movement

The gospels are third-generation remembrances of what happened in the first generation of the Jesus movement. It is important to consider, then, the role of memory in the composition of narratives about the past. One area that has received a great deal of attention in recent research is "collective" or "social" memory. Collective memory is the remembrance of a group. This type of memory is to be distinguished from individual or "autobiographical" memory and "historical" memory.[12] According to Jeffrey Olick:

Autobiographical memory is memory of those events that we ourselves experience (though those experiences are shaped by group memberships), while historical memory is memory that reaches us only through historical records. History is the remembered past to which we no longer have an "organic" relation—the past that is no longer an important part of our lives—while collective memory is the active past that forms our identities.[13]

Neither autobiographical nor collective (social) memory is simply a recollection of the data of the past. Collective memory is that remembrance of the past that is useful to groups in present circumstances. Memory theorists tell us that memories develop or preserve identity, they are contestable, and they are malleable or changeable.[14] Memories develop or preserve identities by focusing on elements of the past that are useful for the present. All groups, from families to nations, use memory in this way. The groups to which we belong tell us which things are important to remember. Christian families celebrate Christmas, while Jews and Muslims do not. The collective memory of many citizens of the United States includes the "Founding Fathers," those Americans of European ancestry who "founded" the nation. The social memory of Native American tribes goes back to a time long before Europeans arrived on this continent. A second feature of social memory is that is contestable. Residents of the United States who are of Mexican ancestry might understand the history of westward expansion of the United States' government quite differently than those of European descent.[15] A final feature of social memory is that social memory is malleable. The understanding of a past shared by a group may change over time as some elements become less useful for the present.

Social memory involves creating narratives of the past that, while malleable, are coherent stories that make sense of information from the past for use by present societies. Frequently, such memories are articulated within certain preestablished literary forms. People tend to tell stories in ways that are common within their cultural settings. Literary genres, therefore, can facilitate the construction of social memories. The gospels are social memories of third-generation Jesus groups that make sense of the story of Jesus for the communities who produce and use such stories to establish and maintain their identities as loyal followers of Jesus in diverse contexts.[16] The gospels do not, however, tell identical stories about Jesus. "Each version had a different general purpose that satisfied third-generation requirement to learn the story of its origins and to find meaning in its details."[17] Even among the closely related Synoptic Gospels, then, we see some significant differences in terms of what is remembered and how it is remembered. These texts are social memories of the groups that produced them.

Several elements of the characterization of Peter are very similar among the three portraits found in the Synoptic Gospels, while each of the three portraits varies somewhat from the others. Careful attention to the details of the characterization of Peter in these three gospels will allow us to see how these differences are shaped by the stories the authors tell about Jesus and his followers. We will also want to know how these portrayals of Peter cohere with the portrayal of Peter found in Paul's letters and what they tell us about the interest in Peter among third-generation Jesus groups.

The Gospel of Mark

In the earliest Synoptic Gospel, Peter is introduced in Mark 1:16. Simon, as he is called before Jesus gives him the nickname "Peter," is a fisherman and has a brother named Andrew. Initially this does not seem like much information, but in terms of the stereotypes of the first-century Galilean world, this information tells us much more than it seems. Simon is a fisherman. The identification of his livelihood reveals quite a bit about who he is.

While modern American social life has four separate social domains (kinship, politics, economy, and religion), first-century Galilee had only two distinct social domains: kinship and politics.[18] Religion and economics were embedded into the political and kinship domains. Kinship, or domestic, economy related to everything families or extended kinship networks produced and consumed. In advanced agrarian societies, households are units of both consumption and production. Domestic religion is the religion of the household or kinship group. It is the honoring of the gods/ancestors that have provided well-being and support to the members of the particular household. Actual kinship groups, that is, biological relatives and their households (including slaves) developed their own domestic religion. Some groups of people who were not related or did not share the same household, however, lived as kinship groups. These groups are called fictive kinship groups. Political economy refers primarily to the elites extracting taxes from the peasant population and making war on rival groups or territories. Political economy was organized to benefit the elite and extract as much as possible of the "surplus" of the peasants. Political religion is the religion of the polity, the larger group of people collected under ethnic auspices (i.e., Israelites honor the God of Israel, while Romans honor the gods of the Roman pantheon). The purpose of political religion is to honor the gods who provide protection and power to the ethnic group. Political religion was usually funded and controlled by the elites of cities or ethnic groups; therefore, political religion, similarly to political economy, represented the interests of such elites.

Galilee in the first century CE was an advanced agrarian economy.[19] Such economies are characterized by small groups of elites, together with those who serve them directly (retainers), ruling over the vast majority of the population, which is comprised of peasant laborers. From the elite perspective, those who made their living fishing were not figures of high repute in ancient Galilee.[20] Fishermen, both those who owned their boats and those who were hired as day laborers or seasonal laborers, "were 'peasants' in the broad sense, since they both live from their work in the boats."[21] As such, their place in the political economy of the Herodian tetrarchy of Galilee, like other peasants, was survival at the level of subsistence with heavy tax burdens. Peter is by no means a person of high status or a wealthy person in the political economy of ancient Galilee.

From Mark's account in 1:16-20, it is unclear whether Peter is fishing from the shore or from a boat. The Greek word (*diktua*) for nets here is a generic word for nets and lacks specificity as to whether it is a type of net that one throws from the shoreline or casts out from a boat.[22] In any case, Mark uses the term "immediately" to describe Simon's action, together with his brother Andrew, in following Jesus (Mark 1:18), noting that they left their nets in order to do so. Simon is one of four men commanded by Jesus to follow him in the opening scene of Jesus' public ministry in the Gospel of Mark. He is there from the beginning of Jesus' Galilean activity, recruited to Jesus' faction by Jesus himself.

Peter's leaving to follow Jesus tells us at least two things about Peter. The first is that Peter is willing to be part of Jesus' movement, the purpose of which, according to Mark, was the call to repentance and the proclamation of the kingdom of God (Mark 1:14-15). The second thing we know about Peter is that he is willing to break with his kinship network. To follow Jesus would mean to leave his kinship group behind. This faction's political purpose (to spread the news regarding the forthcoming theocracy) necessitated a break with the kinship network. The break with his kinship network was due to his traveling with Jesus. He left the occupation of fishing in order to participate in Jesus' movement, thereby failing to secure a food supply for his family.

The next scene in Mark takes place in the house of Simon and Andrew (1:29-31). The fact that the house is described as that of both Simon and Andrew likely indicates that it is the household of their father. It is there that Jesus heals Simon's mother-in-law of a fever (1:31). There is no mention of Peter's wife, nor is his mother-in-law ever referred to again in the gospel. Simon does, in fact, return home if this house is the one that is described in Mark 2:4 and 3:19, but nothing is ever mentioned about his wife or his family again. The story also provides a first depiction of Jesus as a healer, something in which Peter will later participate as a member of Jesus' faction (Mark 6:6b-13).

The next episode in Mark, without parallel in Matthew or Luke, shows Simon (Peter) and his companions searching for Jesus. Jesus had gone alone to pray in a deserted area, and Simon and his companions find Jesus (Mark 1:36-39). The purpose of the story in Mark is to establish the necessity of travel to the other village towns (compare Luke 4:42-43). That Simon (Peter) is the only named individual and the others are called his "companions" (in Greek literally, "the ones with him") indicate that Peter is already becoming a central person in Jesus' network.

In Mark 3:13-19, Jesus appoints twelve followers "whom he wanted" (3:13). Simon is listed first, and it is at this point that the reader is informed that Jesus gave to Simon the name Peter (3:16). Giving Peter a new name implies Jesus' power and authority over him. Patrons and masters gave new names to their clients and slaves, respectively. To provide a new name signals entry into Jesus' faction.[23] This selection of the Twelve signals the beginning of Jesus' faction. A faction is "a group of people gathered by some central person for a given time to assist the faction founder in his project."[24] In this case, the faction is a group centered on Jesus as a central person whose purpose is the proclamation of the forthcoming theocracy.

Membership in this faction comes with certain responsibilities and privileges. As part of the faction, Peter received private teaching regarding the meaning of the parables (Mark 4:10-20). Peter also witnessed deeds of power that are witnessed by few others, including the majority of the disciples (Mark 5:35-43). The members of Jesus' faction carry forward Jesus' program by casting out unclean spirits and healing the sick (6:6-13). The purposes of the faction are to spread the word of the forthcoming theocracy and to recruit members to the coalition of those preparing for the theocracy. This carrying forward of the program of the faction involves travel, entailing the disciples' leaving their kinship groups (Mark 10:28).

Peter is next mentioned by name in the narrative when Jesus questions his disciples concerning his reputation. This scene, traditionally conceived of as Peter's "confession," is a discussion about Jesus' reputation outside the group and within his group. Richard Rohrbaugh argues that this text is not about Peter "getting it right" concerning Jesus' identity in the gospel.[25] In a collectivist society, Jesus' question deals with his reputation. He asks the disciples what people say about him. His public identity comes from the understandings others have of him, as one would expect in a collective society. In this instance, Peter answers for the ingroup. Jesus, according to his disciples, is "Messiah," the anointed agent of God. Jesus' question, answered by Peter, is addressed to the disciples collectively. The plural for "you" is used in 8:29, and Peter answers for the group. That the answer represents the group collectively is confirmed by Jesus' charge to all of the disciples not to speak about him to anyone (8:31).

When Jesus first tells the disciples about his fate, Peter rebukes Jesus. Jesus' response to Peter shows an element of Peter's character in the gospel that foreshadows Peter's denial of Jesus. Peter does not accept Jesus' fate, though Jesus himself seems fully willing to accept such a fate. The three passion predictions (Mark 8:31; 9:31; 10:33-34) and Jesus' prayer at Gethsemane (14:32-40) alert the reader to the fact that Jesus goes willingly, if perhaps reluctantly in the Gethsemane account, to his fate. The three passion predictions show an ever-widening confusion on the part of those who follow Jesus. In the first instance, Peter rebukes Jesus, but in the second passion prediction it is the disciples as a group who do not understand what Jesus is saying (Mark 9:32). Peter's rebuke of Jesus, which in turn earns him a rebuke when Jesus calls him "Satan" and tells him that he is setting his "mind not on divine things but on human things" (Mark 8:33), parallels the lack of understanding and fear of the entire group of disciples in the second passion prediction (Mark 9:32). Immediately prior to the final passion prediction, "those who followed" Jesus "were afraid" (Mark 10:32). This group of people following Jesus includes a number larger than the twelve disciples because Jesus takes the Twelve aside after the description of the amazement and fear of those who followed him (Mark 10:32). To further parallel Peter's rebuke and Jesus' response in the first passion prediction, after each of the passion predictions Jesus redefines what it means to achieve honor in his faction: it is to deny oneself (Mark 8:34-38), to welcome children (9:33-37), and to drink from the cup of Jesus' suffering (10:35-40), which leads to service toward all in the community on the model of Jesus' service (10:41-45). In the account of Peter's rebuke of Jesus and Jesus' rebuke of Peter, Peter clearly represents the group of disciples. He is leader by virtue of his willingness to respond to Jesus' passion prediction. Peter is well established as the leader of the group of disciples when taken with his response on behalf of the group to Jesus' question concerning his identity in Mark 8:29.

Peter plays a significant role at the transfiguration of Jesus (9:2-8). Like at the raising of Jairus' daughter (Mark 5:35-43), Peter is one of a group of three taken separately from the Twelve who is witness to an event to which the others are not privy. Here again the group of three consists of Peter, James, and John (9:2). Sensing that it is a good place to be, Peter proposes building three tents, one for Jesus, one for Moses, and one for Elijah (9:5). Here again Peter is a representative of the group, as Mark's editorial comment in 9:6 informs the reader. Peter "did not know what to say, for they were terrified." The fear (Gk: *ekphobos*) had fallen upon all three of them, but only Peter speaks in his ignorance born from fright. It is interesting to note that Peter here is described as "afraid," the same description given for his actions in Galatians 2:11-14.

The next time Peter is mentioned individually in Mark it is to remind Jesus of the things that the disciples have given up to follow Jesus (Mark 10:28). This remark by Peter follows Jesus' assertion that it is exceedingly difficult for the rich to enter the kingdom of God (10:23-27). Peter here is attempting to ensure his (and the other disciples') place in the patronage network of God. Jesus spoke of God as a heavenly patron who is able to provide for his clients, including Jesus' disciples. Jesus reassures him that those who have removed themselves from the kinship and patronage networks will be rewarded "a hundredfold now in this age—houses, brothers and sisters, mothers and children, and fields, with persecutions—and in the age to come eternal life" (Mark 10:30). Peter has a secure place in the patronage network of God, of which Jesus is a broker and Peter is a subbroker (see Mark 6:6b-11). This point is reinforced by Peter's remark concerning the withered fig tree (Mark 11:21). Jesus' response is that those faithful to God will receive "whatever you for ask in prayer" (11:24). The promise of houses, siblings, mothers, children, and fields might already represent third-generation interests. It indicates a strong concern with fictive family relationships that are not part of the immediate proclamation of the kingdom of God. The promise of houses, family members, and fields fits more easily into the concerns of the third generation who did not expect the immediate arrival of God's rule.

Peter, together with James, John, and Andrew, receives one more private teaching in Mark's gospel. In 13:3-4, they ask Jesus to tell them about the signs that precede the arrival of God's kingdom. Jesus lists a number of events that will precede the arrival of the kingdom (13:5-31) but tells them that he does not know the day or hour of the coming of the kingdom (13:32). Even the broker of God's benefaction does not know everything concerning the heavenly Patron's beneficence. This lack of specificity also likely represents the concerns of the third generation.

Peter plays a relatively substantial role in the passion narrative. Unfortunately for Peter, the reasons for his prominence are largely due to his denial of Jesus (Mark 14:66-72). Leading up to the denials, Peter features prominently in two scenes. After the final meal of Jesus with his disciples, Jesus predicts that his followers "will all become deserters" (14:27).[26] Peter insists that he will not become a deserter, and Jesus responds by telling him that "this day, this very night, before the cock crows twice, you will deny me three times" (14:30). Peter rebuts Jesus, asserting that he will remain faithful even to his death (14:31).

The next episode features Peter asleep three times in Gethsemane while Jesus goes to pray (14:32-42). The first time Jesus returns from prayer, he singles out Simon for sleeping, asking whether he could "not keep awake one hour" (14:37). Even the leader is unable to keep watch to safeguard Jesus. At the arrest of Jesus, the reader of the gospel is told "All of them deserted him and fled" (14:50). Peter, however, continues to follow Jesus "at a distance, right into the courtyard of the high priest" (14:54). When one of the high priest's female slaves recognizes him as a follower of Jesus, Peter denies knowing what she says (14:68). At this point the author of the text increases the physical distance between Peter and Jesus by relating that Peter "went out into the forecourt" (14:68). The female slave, however, tells the public that Peter is "one of them" (14:69). Peter again denies it, and the bystanders challenge his denial because of his Galilean ethnicity. Peter denies even knowing Jesus at that point (14:71). Peter wept upon hearing the cock crow a second time (14:72). This episode is the last in which Peter plays a part in the Gospel of Mark.

The crowd identifies Peter as a follower of Jesus due to his ethnic identity. Ancient Mediterranean people were accustomed to using broad generalizations about members of various ethnic groups. Because of the stereotyping inherent in collectivist cultures, there is a general attitude that knowing one member of an ethnic group is equivalent to knowing them all.[27] This type of stereotyping is preserved clearly in the New Testament in Titus 1:12 ("Cretans are always liars, vicious brutes, lazy gluttons"). We do not know how the crowd in the high priest's courtyard identified Peter as Galilean, but there are a number of possibilities. Clothing, speech, or physical mannerisms might have identified Peter as such.

There is one further mention of his name in Mark 16:7. The young man at the tomb tells the women to "go, tell his disciples and Peter that he is going ahead of you to Galilee; there you will see him, just as he told you." Peter here again is singled out, this time due to the fact that he had denied Jesus. The narrative ends on a note of optimism, however, in that Peter is to be included in the ones to see Jesus in Galilee.

There are positive and negative characteristics of Peter displayed in the Gospel of Mark. He is a peasant fisherman who joins the faction of Jesus and becomes the leader and spokesperson for the group of disciples in the Gospel of Mark. He receives private teaching and witnesses deeds of power, including the raising of Jairus' daughter; he spreads the message regarding the kingdom of God; and he heals people and casts out unclean spirits. He is not a person who behaves in a consistent manner, acting out of fear at the transfiguration, immediately preceding the third passion prediction, and presumably (though it is not explicitly stated) from the same motive in denying Jesus. At crucial moments, especially in rebuking Jesus after Jesus announces his fate, falling asleep in Gethsemane, and denying Jesus, Peter lacks loyalty to Jesus.

The Gospel of Matthew

Matthew's gospel uses Mark as a basic source for the narrative. In the majority of cases, the Markan material concerning Peter is passed on without significant change, but there are some minor modifications in Matthew's account, and there are four instances in Matthew in which Peter is mentioned that have no direct parallel in Mark. We begin with a discussion of some of the minor changes found in Matthew. The initial encounter between Simon and Jesus is very similar to the account found in Mark. The only difference is that Matthew tells the reader at this stage in the story that Simon already has the nickname Peter (Matt 4:18). This does not necessarily mean that the author is unaware that Jesus is supposed to have given the nickname to Peter, but it may imply that. Other Matthean sections that are very similar to the Markan accounts are Peter's rebuke of Jesus and Jesus' rebuke of Peter after the first passion prediction (16:21-23), Peter's assertion that he and the other disciples have left everything to follow Jesus (17:1-9), Peter's prediction that he will not desert Jesus (26:33-35), Peter's falling asleep in Gethsemane and failing to keep watch (26:36-46), and Peter's following Jesus into the courtyard of the high priest's house and subsequently denying Jesus three times (26:58, 69-75). Though there are slight differences in the Matthean and Markan accounts of Peter's denial,[28] these differences do not substantially change the characterization of Peter.

Some events reported in both Mark and Matthew show somewhat greater differences. Matthew places the healing of Peter's mother-in-law after the Sermon on the Mount, and it is the first of a cycle of deeds of power in this gospel (Matt 8–9). According to Matthew's text, Jesus sees Peter's mother-in-law rather than being told about her (Matt 8:14). Matthew's naming of the twelve disciples is somewhat different than Mark's account. In Mark, Jesus selects the Twelve and they are named in the text. Matthew's account (10:1-4) relates that "Jesus summoned his twelve disciples" (10:1). The disciples here already constitute a group of twelve, though Matthew does not describe how they were so designated. Peter is described as the "first" of the disciples (10:2). His leadership of the group is made explicit with this designation.

Sometimes the author of Matthew omits Peter's name where it occurs in Mark's text. Instead of listing only Peter, James, and John as witnesses to the raising of Jairus' daughter (Matt 9:18-26), the whole group of twelve witnesses this deed of power (Matt 9:19). The fig tree incident is different in Matthew's gospel since the curse occurs after the cleansing of the temple and results in the immediate withering of the fig tree. In Mark, Peter is the one to ask about the tree, but in Matthew the immediate withering prompts the "disciples," not Peter specifically, to ask, "How did the fig tree wither at once?" (Matt 21:20). The disciples as a group, rather than the quartet of Peter, James, John, and Andrew, inquire about the sign of the coming and the end of the age (Matt 24:3). Finally, Matthew omits the addition of "and Peter" to the announcement to the women by the angel of Lord after Jesus is raised (Matt 28:7).

Most significant for understanding the character of Peter in Matthew's gospel are those texts that either add substantially to the Markan account or do not appear in Mark's gospel at all.

There is one incident that is significantly expanded, and there are four incidents in Matthew that do not occur at all in Mark. The "confession" of Peter is significantly expanded by Matthew (Matt 16:16-20). Jesus makes a reply to Peter's confession, "Blessed are you, Simon son of Jonah! For flesh and blood has not revealed this to you, but my father in heaven" (Matt 16:17). Two additional bits of information are given about Peter that are not found in Mark's text. First, Simon's father (Jonah) is mentioned here. Second, Peter is a recipient of heavenly wisdom from God. There is nothing in Mark's text, nor is there anything else in Matthew's text, to indicate that Peter is given divine wisdom except through the brokerage of Jesus. Jesus goes on to say, "You are Peter, and on this rock I will build my church, and the gates of Hades will not prevail against it. I will give you the keys of the kingdom of heaven, and whatever you bind on earth will be bound in heaven, and whatever you loose on earth will be loosed in heaven" (Matt 16:18-19).[29] Peter's role as the head of the group of disciples is surely the reason for his being given authority to bind and loose, an authority that in Matthew 18:18 is given to all of the disciples, and it seems, by extension, to any member of this community (Gk: *ekklēsia*; Matt 18:15-20). In other words, the authority granted to Peter in Matthew 16:18-19 is not granted to Peter alone but is extended to all those faithful to Jesus.

Jesus' saying "you are Peter" might indicate that, like Mark, Matthew understood Jesus to have given Peter this name. The text is unclear on this point, especially since Matthew 4:18 and 10:2 already refer to "Simon, who is called Peter." The verse sets up a wordplay on Peter's nickname, "Rocky" (Gk: *Petros*), and the word "rock" (Gk: *petra*). That wordplay is likely the reason that his nickname is mentioned at this point.

Peter also receives the "keys of the kingdom of heaven" (Matt 16:19). This saying is not repeated in Matthew 18:18. The keys belong to Peter alone, likely as the head of the disciples. The saying regarding the keys confers to Peter "access to God's benefaction; Peter would be a broker like Jesus."[30] It also seems that the community that produced Matthew's gospel saw Peter's teaching as the foundation stone of their community (Matt 16:18).

As in Mark, Peter and the other disciples receive private teaching that the crowd does not receive. Peter asks for an explanation of the "parable" of the saying regarding the things that defile (Matt 15:10-19). This saying and its explanation follow Jesus' rebuke of the scribes and Pharisees for the way in which they observe Judean traditions. The issue for Jesus' faction is not whether to observe Judean customs but how they should be observed. The very point of the Sermon on the Mount is that Jesus' disciples observe Judean customs more stringently than other Judeans. Pheme Perkins calls this explanation of the saying "particularly significant because it follows a discussion between Jesus and his disciples about the authority of the Pharisees."[31] For Matthew, then, "Peter (and the other disciples) will not be blind guides leading the people to disaster."[32] Peter, and the other followers of Jesus, will instead lead the followers of Jesus to the type of purity necessary as preparation for God's forthcoming rule.

In another instance of private teaching, Jesus tells Peter he is to forgive a sinning sibling in the community "seventy-seven times" (Matt 18:22). After Jesus' discussion of right behavior toward other members of the community, Peter alone came to him (Matt 18:21). Peter's standing as the leader of the disciples is further elaborated in the question regarding the temple tax. The tax collectors come to Peter to inquire about whether Jesus' followers pay the temple tax (Matt 17:24). Peter is known as the leader of the group even outside the ingroup. Access to Jesus and his teaching, then, is brokered by Peter to those outside the group, in this case, tax collectors. Peter is a central figure in Jesus' network (compare Mark 1:36-39).

There is also the further episode in which Peter walks on water. Peter's walk upon the Sea of Galilee is added to Mark's tradition (Mark 6:45-52). Peter asks Jesus to command him to leave the boat and walk on the water (Matt 14:28). Peter begins walking on the sea, but then he "became frightened, and beginning to sink, he cried out, "Lord, save me!" (Matt 14:30). Again

Peter's behavior changes when he is overcome with fear. This episode, though not recorded in Mark's gospel, preserves the tradition that Peter's behavior can change radically due to fear. Peter even earns the rebuke from Jesus, "You of little faith, why did you doubt?" (Matt 14:31).

The final scene in the Gospel of Matthew brings Peter's character full circle. In Mark, there is the promise of a meeting with the risen Jesus in Galilee (Mark 16:7). Matthew narrates such a meeting between Jesus and the eleven remaining disciples, excluding Judas, who hanged himself (Matt 28:16-20). Jesus commissions the disciples to "make disciples of all nations [Gk: *ehtnē*], baptizing them in the name of the Father and of the Son and of the Holy Spirit, and teaching them to obey everything that I have commanded you" (Matt 28:19-20). Significantly, Peter is not singled out from the group at this stage. In Matthew's gospel, Jesus is a new lawgiver (see especially the Sermon on the Mount), and the disciples bear the burden of teaching and enforcing the commandments of Jesus after his death. That the disciples are here told to baptize and teach observation of Jesus' commandments represents third-generation interests. The first-generation members of Jesus' movement were to proclaim the theocracy, heal, and exorcise (Matt 10:7-8).

The portrait of Peter in the Gospel of Matthew is similar in many ways to the description of Peter in the Gospel of Mark. The Matthean material that is not found in Mark serves to highlight Peter's role as the leader of the group and the recipient of private teaching but also as a character whose fear sometimes gets the best of him. Peter is a character flawed by his inability consistently to follow Jesus.

The Gospel of Luke

Peter's call in Luke's narrative occurs slightly later than his call in Mark. In Mark's text, calling Peter and Andrew is Jesus' first action upon entering Galilee after his baptism and the temptation in the Judean desert. In Luke, however, Jesus calls Peter only after having given his initial address in the synagogue at Nazareth (Luke 4:16-30). The address in the synagogue at Nazareth functions in Luke as the impetus for Jesus' first entry into Capernaum (Luke 4:31). There is a significant divergence between Luke's story of Jesus' early interaction with Simon and Mark's account. Mark gives no indication that the two figures had known each other prior to Jesus' call to Simon. Luke, on the other hand, narrates the healing of Simon's mother-in-law before Simon becomes Jesus' disciple (Luke 4:38-41). This episode happens after Jesus calls Peter to join his faction in Mark.

The "call" of Peter happens differently in this Gospel as well. Jesus is pressed by the crowd into a boat, "the one belonging to Simon" (Luke 5:3). Though the NRSV indicates that the boat is Simon's, the Greek text here is ambiguous regarding whether the boat belonged to Simon or whether it was the boat from which he normally fished. The following tale of the bountiful catch indicates that Luke envisions Peter and Andrew as part of a fishing cooperative, since they were working with partners who fished from other boats.[33] The miraculous size of the catch compels Peter to extol his unworthiness in the face of Jesus. Such expressions of unworthiness are related to benefactions and the patronage system. Jesus provides access to the benefactions of the God of Israel, who acts as a patron toward Jesus and those in his faction. Simon is indebted to Jesus for his procurement of the sizable catch.[34] He is also indebted to Jesus for restoring his mother-in-law to health from fever (Luke 4:38-39). As soon as they return to shore, they leave their boats and follow Jesus. Luke provides a more compelling set of reasons for Peter to become part of Jesus' movement. Jesus is a broker of heavenly benefactions toward Peter before he becomes Jesus' disciple.

When Jesus designates the twelve disciples in Luke's gospel, he chooses them from among a larger group of disciples (Luke 6:13). These twelve are also called "apostles" by Luke (6:13). As in Mark, these disciples are given authority over demons (Mark reads "unclean spirits") and the command "to proclaim" (Luke

9:1). Luke specifies that the disciples are to proclaim the kingdom of God (9:2). Luke also adds that another task the disciples are to perform is "to cure disease" (9:2), a task not explicitly given the disciples in Mark but one which they nevertheless perform (Mark 6:13).

Several Lukan texts are very similar to or completely identical to their Markan counterparts. Even where minor differences occur, for example, in Luke's account of the raising of Jairus' daughter, Peter's characterization in the story, as one of three disciples to witness the event, is identical to the Markan version (Luke 8:49-56). Peter's "confession" is identical in terms of Peter's characterization. Peter adds to his designation of Jesus as "the Messiah" the words "of God" in Luke 9:20. As in Mark, immediately following this description of Jesus' identity, Jesus tells the disciples what his fate will be (Luke 9:21-22). In Mark, this first passion prediction is followed by Peter's rebuke of Jesus and Jesus' rebuke of Peter (Mark 8:32-33). Both of these rebukes are eliminated in Luke's narrative. Peter does not question Jesus' fate in this gospel. Nor does Luke's Peter, unlike the Peter of Matthew and Mark, deny that he will desert and deny Jesus (Luke 9:33). When he does deny Jesus three times (22:55-62), he also does not curse, nor does he swear an oath insisting that he does not know Jesus.[35]

There are several differences in the Lukan account of Jesus' transfiguration (Luke 9:28-37). As in the Markan account, Peter, James, and John accompany Jesus up the mountain. Luke's account of Jesus' transfiguration occurs while Jesus is at prayer (Luke 9:29). In Luke's version of the account, Elijah and Moses speak with Jesus about "his departure [Gk: *exodos*], which he was about to accomplish at Jerusalem" (9:31). It is only in Luke's account that Peter, James, and John are described as "weighed down with sleep" (9:32), yet since "they had stayed awake, they saw his glory and the two men who stood with him" (9:32). Peter, as in the Markan account, notes that it is good for them to be there and offers to make three dwellings (9:33). Peter only offers to make these dwellings, however, "as they [Elijah and

Moses] were leaving him" (9:33). Unlike the Markan and Matthean versions of the account, Jesus does not order the disciples to silence. Luke says the disciples themselves told no one of it "in those days" (9:36). The addition of "in those days" surely is meant to preserve the idea of Peter, James, and John as witnesses to the event who told others at some later point (see Luke 24:48).

In the Gospel of Luke, even more than in the Gospel of Matthew, Peter's leadership role and status in the Jesus faction are given precedence.[36] This status is shown clearly in the account of Jesus' instructions to Peter on the night of his arrest in the Garden of Gethsemane. Jesus, who prays only one time in Gethsemane in Luke, tells Peter, "Simon, Simon, listen! Satan has demanded to sift all of you like wheat, but I have prayed for you that your own faith may not fail; and you, when once you have turned back, strengthen your brothers" (Luke 22:31-32). Peter will be the one to reconvene the group and carry forth the work of the kingdom after Jesus' death and resurrection. The account of this plays out in two ways. Luke adds a resurrection appearance to Peter not contained in Mark or Matthew (Luke 24:12). In Mark, the women do not announce the words of the young man to the disciples because they are afraid (Mark 16:7). In Matthew, the women do relate the message of the angel, and the disciples regroup on the mountain in Galilee where Jesus appears to them (Matt 28:7-8, 16-20). In Luke's account, there are two men who tell the women that Jesus has been raised (24:5-7). Remembering what Jesus had said (presumably in the passion predictions), they "told all this to the eleven and to all the rest" (24:9). Peter, unlike the others who considered the words "an idle tale, and . . . did not believe them" (24:11), "got up and ran to the tomb; stooping and looking in, he saw the linen cloths by themselves; then he went home, amazed at what had happened" (24:12). The two disciples on the road to Emmaus also report to "the eleven and their companions gathered together" that the "Lord has risen indeed, and he has appeared to Simon!" (24:33-34). This appearance to Simon is not narrated beyond that brief description in Luke 24:34, but the idea that the resurrected Jesus appeared to Simon before the other disciples is consistent with Paul's description in 1 Corinthians 15.

The priority of Peter, especially in Jesus' words to him in Gethsemane and in the resurrection appearance to him, established Peter as the leader designated to reconstitute the group after Jesus' resurrection. In the second volume of Luke's account, Peter plays this role for the Jerusalem Jesus movement as he becomes broker of God's benefactions by virtue of his possession of the Holy Spirit and his bold speech.

A Note on John

John's gospel is in many ways similar to the Synoptics in its portrayal of Peter. There are a few minor differences, however, and a few larger differences. Simon Peter is recruited to the movement by his brother Andrew rather than directly by Jesus (John 1:42-43). Peter is from Bethsaida in this gospel rather than Capernaum (John 1:44). There are really three major differences between John and the Synoptics. Peter's "confession" comes after Jesus' speech about the Bread of Life (John 6). Major differences are found in the fact that Peter's role at the last meal with Jesus is expanded when he initially refuses to allow Jesus to wash his feet and then insists that Jesus wash his hands and head as well (John 13:6-10), and that Peter is the one who strikes the slave's ear in the Garden of Gethsemane (John 18:10). The most profound difference is that Peter is not the "leader" of the disciples, but he is subordinate in many ways to the disciple whom Jesus loves (John 13:24; 18:15-16; 20:2-9). There may be reasons for this contrast between Peter and the Beloved Disciple that extend to the relationship between the community that produced this gospel and the one that produced Luke's gospel.[37] The memory of Peter in John is one of a disciple who is somewhat less than the ideal, the Beloved Disciple.

Memories of Peter in the
Third Generation of the Jesus Movement

Several things are clear about Peter's reputation in the third generation of the Jesus movement. By the time of the composition of Mark and Matthew, Peter's reputation was as one who lacked the constancy of an ideal follower. He is motivated by fear in both gospels at certain key points (notably when he walks on the water and presumably when he denies knowing Jesus). This characterization of Peter mirrors Paul's characterization of Peter found in Galatians. The significance of Peter's role among the Twelve, however, is also notable in these two gospels. He is always the first named in the lists of disciples; he is privy to much private teaching; he witnesses a number of miraculous events; and he is sent, along with the other disciples, to proclaim Jesus' message, heal, and cast out unclean spirits. This type of portrait of Peter coheres rather nicely with that painted by Paul in 1 Corinthians.

In Luke, Peter's portrayal is much more unambiguous. There is no motivation of fear, and his lack of fidelity to Jesus in his denials is determined by the outside force of Satan operating upon him. Despite his denials, however, he is the first of the disciples to see the risen Jesus, and he becomes the undisputed leader of the group in Jerusalem in Acts. Peter's character is, in Luke's gospel, one of constancy, and he has been prepared to become the broker of heavenly benefits from God through Jesus to the earthly followers of Jesus.

CHAPTER 4

Peter after Jesus' Ascension

In Acts, Peter takes on and fulfills a number of the roles performed by Jesus in the Gospel of Luke. Like Jesus, Peter receives the Holy Spirit along with the other disciples of Jesus (Acts 2:1-4), preaches with a special focus on interpreting Scripture (especially Acts 2:14-36), heals (Acts 3:1-9), arouses the anger of the high priest (Acts 5:17-42), and hears a heavenly voice from parted heavens (Acts 10:9-16). Peter is able to do these things because he is possessed by the Holy Spirit, which provides him with the ability to interpret Scripture and to speak with the "boldness" (Gk: *parrēsia*) characteristic of him in the text.

Peter performs two different roles in Acts: holy man and moral entrepreneur. These roles describe Peter's leadership among the ingroup of Jesus' disciples and his role as a witness beyond the group of Jesus' disciples. In Luke 22:31-32, Jesus told Peter "Simon, Simon, listen! Satan has demanded to sift all of you [plural] like wheat, but I have prayed for you [singular] that your [singular] own faith may not fail; and you [singular], when once you [singular] have turned back, strengthen your brothers." Peter's role as the one to strengthen the "brothers" acknowledges his standing at the forefront of the group.[1] Jesus' prayer for Peter, given his knowledge that the whole group of disciples will undergo this "sifting," is particularly significant for understanding Peter's roles in the book of Acts.

Peter's Social Status in the Book of Acts

In Acts, Peter is described as "unlettered" (Gk: *agrammatos*) and "ordinary" (Gk: *idiotēs*; 4:13). This depiction of Peter (applied in Acts 4 also to John) describes him as a low-status figure. The description of Peter in Acts 4:13 makes sense in the context of his social status as a first-century Galilean fisherman, discussed in chapter 3 above. There is very little reason to suppose that Peter would have been able to read and write. Despite his being uneducated, however, he speaks "boldly" (Gk: *parrēsia*). *Parrēsia* is a type of speech that is critical and frank. It is normally expected from true friends (as opposed to flatterers) and often from philosophers who are especially critical of elites and rulers.[2] Such frankness bears the marks of fearlessness. Peter, in Acts, is no longer afraid but speaks boldly even to those who oppose him. Peter is behaving in a manner that would not be expected from someone of his status, and "the priests, the captain of the temple, and the Sadducees" (4:1) attempt to shame him and John by labeling them deviants. The response to Peter's healing of the crippled beggar (3:1-10) is that the crowd "praised God for what had happened" (4:21). The disciples' response to the events of the day is to pray to "speak your word with all boldness" (4:29). Both of these notices are meant to portray Peter and John as the winners of the honor challenge between themselves and the temple leadership. The disciples' reputations are enhanced, and the temple leadership is unable to prevent them from continuing to perform activities that the leaders deem unacceptable.

The description of Peter as unlettered and ordinary highlights all the more the significance of his being a powerful orator who speaks with boldness, persuading those to whom he speaks.

Perhaps even more striking, however, is that Peter fulfills functions normally associated with scribes. He is an interpreter of Scripture, not only citing Scripture, but providing its interpretation. Peter's actions in this book, including his skills in rhetoric and scriptural interpretation, are due to his possession by the Holy Spirit in the same way that Jesus is possessed of this Spirit in the Gospel of Luke. Peter is possessed by the Spirit in two cases in which he interprets Scripture for the people of Jerusalem (including his adversaries). In the first instance (Acts 2:14-36), the Spirit has been granted to the disciples (2:1-4). When they hear the disciples speaking in tongues, some of the bystanders think that they are drunk (2:13). Peter interprets Scripture to argue that the behavior of the disciples is consistent with the promise of the Spirit in the last days (2:17). Peter also interprets Scripture (4:8-12) when he is brought for a hearing in front of the rulers, elders, scribes, and several members of priestly families (4:5). Just before he begins to speak in his defense, Peter is described as "filled with the Holy Spirit" (4:8). The possession of the Spirit is an indication of Peter's status as a holy man in Acts.

Peter as Holy Person: Altered States of Consciousness

Holy people share a number of characteristics. Among the most prominent of these characteristics is accessibility to the realm of the divine through experiences of altered states of consciousness. Several accounts in the book of Acts are best described as alternate-states-of-consciousness experiences. Such states "may be defined as a temporary change in the overall pattern of subjective experience, such that the individual believes that his or her mental functioning is distinctly different from certain general norms for his or her normal waking state of consciousness."[3] Perhaps the most famous New Testament example is Paul's vision of the risen Jesus on the road to Damascus (Acts 9:1-9). This event fits into "a pattern of a personal encounter in an alternate state of consciousness" found in Acts.[4] Altered-states-of-consciousness experiences (hereafter, ASCs) are common in most culture groups of the world even today.[5] ASCs vary widely and include as many as twenty different states of consciousness. "Altered sates of consciousness shade one into another and are notoriously difficult to define. They may, however, be thought of as ranging along a continuum. At one end of the continuum we have what we may loosely call 'alert consciousness'; at the other end is deep trance."[6] ASCs are "conditions in which sensations, perceptions, cognition and emotion are altered."[7]

It is sometimes difficult for modern North Americans to appreciate what ASCs are and how they work. Cultures that acknowledge ASCs as regular occurrences are called polyphasic cultures, while North American cultures tend to be monophasic.[8] Monophasic cultures are those in which people are socialized to "rely solely on the waking state of consciousness for obtaining knowledge about themselves and the world," whereas in polyphasic cultures "ASCs manifest themselves regularly within religious or cultural rituals as cultivated means of producing knowledge about the world that is appreciated by the community."[9] John Pilch notes, "In our scientific minded culture, the latent discourse responds with skepticism to any altered states of consciousness experiences. Indeed, ASCs are often considered to be pathological or signs of pathology."[10] In ancient Mediterranean cultures, however, the latent discourse of the culture cued people to describe such experiences as meetings with beings from the realm of God (or the gods).[11] These ASC experiences can be part of what Pieter Craffert labels the "shamanic complex." He divides the types of activities in which shamans participate into two types: "on the one hand, healer and controller of spirits and, on the other hand, divinator and educator."[12] Peter participates in each of these types of activities in the book of Acts.

Pilch notes four major types of ASC experiences that are prevalent in the world of the New Testament: "(1) healing, that is, restoration of meaning to life (e.g., Acts 3:4); (2) divination, that is, seeking or learning the answer to a question or solution to a problem (e.g., Acts 16:9-10); (3) metamorphosis, the blurring of the boundaries between the human world and the realm of God in hopes of learning how to work change that is needed and/or desired (e.g., Acts 12:6-11); (4) and sky (or spirit) journeys."[13] This fourth type of ASC involves "visits to the realm of God."[14] Such sky journeys occur in the biblical texts in Isaiah 6 and Revelation 4 among other places. Paul refers to one such experience in 2 Corinthians 12:1-5.[15] Though such sky journeys can be a regular feature of the experience of holy people, Peter does not undertake such a sky journey in the book of Acts.

Holy people are considered to have "privileged and facile access to the spirit realm" and the "ability to broker favors from that realm to needy human beings."[16] Peter is part of the group of disciples to whom Jesus appeared over a period of forty days after which "he was taken up to heaven" (Acts 1:2). Peter and the others are witnesses to the resurrection of Jesus because "he presented himself alive to them by many convincing proofs" (Acts 1:3). This encounter with the risen Jesus is an ASC experience.[17] Peter and the others see Jesus in a group trance.[18] There are numerous means for entering into trance states, among which are various types of mental illness, use of psychotropic drugs, "sensory deprivation . . . prolonged social isolation, intense pain, vigorous dancing, and insistent, rhythmic sound, such as drumming or chanting."[19] Another method for entering a trance state is prayer. "In trance or in any other alternate state of consciousness, a person encounters, indeed enters, another level or aspect of reality registered physiologically in the brain in the same way 'normal' experiences are."[20]

When the disciples see the risen Jesus, they naturally assume he is a messenger from the realm of God. This experience is a group trance. Jesus explains to them that they are to be witnesses to him (Acts 1:8). In this sense, their role as witnesses is the same as that of Paul after his encounter with the risen Jesus (Acts 22:15) or of Stephen, who also had a vision of the risen Jesus (Acts

7:54-60). In addition to seeing Jesus ascend into the realm of God, the disciples see two other heavenly beings explaining what they have seen to them (Acts 1:11).[21] This explanation is due in part to the fact that "Every vision, every trance experience needs an explanation."[22] Visions are regularly explained in the book of Acts (see, for example, Acts 1:11; 2:14-36; 9:4-6, 17; 10:17-33).

The second group trance experience related in Acts is the receipt of the Holy Spirit. In this case, the Spirit possesses the disciples and they both hear a "rushing wind" and see "tongues of fire" (Acts 2:2-3). The effects of this group trance experience are made known immediately afterward when the disciples "began to speak in other languages, as the Spirit gave them ability" (Acts 2:4). Possession by the Spirit is a separate type of trance experience from visions, and these types of experiences are common among agricultural societies like that found in first-century Palestine.[23] Possession occurs when "a being of the alternate reality" takes "up its abode in the body of the worshipper itself. . . . It will shake them, make them dance; it might take over their tongues and speak through their mouths."[24] This type of possession by the Spirit is exactly what occurs to the disciples in Acts 2:4. When the Spirit comes upon them, they are given the ability to speak in other languages. It is important to note that, in Luke's account, even those skeptical of the disciples' behavior recognize that their behavior is an ASC. These skeptics suggest that the ASC is drunkenness rather than spirit possession, but all in the audience, whether skeptical or credulous, recognize an ASC. The challenge to the disciples' honor ("They are filled with new wine"; Acts 2:13) prompts a response from Peter that involves Peter's interpreting Scripture. This represents a significant change in Peter's role from the Gospel of Luke to Acts.

In Luke's gospel, Simon Peter never interprets Scripture. In fact, there is an indication in the gospel that Peter misunderstands Jesus when Jesus interprets Scripture. In Luke 24:44-49, when Jesus appears to the disciples after his resurrection, "he opened their minds to understand the scriptures" (24:45). Jesus explained to them that "everything written about me in the law of Moses, the prophets, and the psalms must be fulfilled" (24:44). Jesus told his disciples three times before his crucifixion that he was to die (Luke 9:21-22, 44-45; and 18:31-34), but "they understood nothing about all these things; in fact, what he said was hidden from them, and they did not grasp what was said" (18:34). Peter understands only when, after his resurrection, Jesus explains the meaning of the Scripture as related to his fate. It is somewhat surprising, then, that Peter is a Scripture interpreter *par excellence* in the book of Acts. Peter is able to contextualize Jesus' death and rising in the context of Scripture only after receiving the Spirit at Pentecost. The coming of the Holy Spirit brings with it the same ability to interpret Scripture that Jesus was given in the Gospel of Luke (Luke 4:1, 14-30). This ability follows something of a pattern in Acts. After receiving the Spirit, Stephen interprets Scripture (Acts 7:1-53), as do Philip (8:35) and Paul (13:16b-47). Luke indicates in two different ways that it is the presence of the Spirit that allows Jesus to interpret Scripture. Just before Jesus is tempted by Satan and responds by interpreting Scripture, Luke tells the hearer of his account that Jesus was "full of the Holy Spirit" (Luke 4:1). When Jesus interprets Scripture in the synagogue at Nazareth, his "reading" includes Isaiah 61:1-2, which reads "The Spirit of the Lord is upon me" (Luke 4:18). Jesus gives the interpretation of the saying by stressing, "Today this scripture has been fulfilled in your hearing" (Luke 4:21). Jesus' possession by the Spirit of God gives him the capacity to understand and convey the true meaning of the Scriptures of Israel.

In the same manner, Peter's possession by the Holy Spirit enables him to understand the true meaning of Israel's Scriptures. It is in the ASC that Peter is able to expound the meaning of Scripture. Peter alerts his audience to the fulfillment of the prophecy of Joel regarding the onset of ASC experiences when the "last days" come (Acts 2:17-20). The ability to prophesy in this case has to do with understanding the meaning of the Scriptures, as Jesus explained to Cleopas and another unnamed follower on the road to Emmaus (Luke 24:27). As Jesus in Luke, so Peter in Acts 2:17-36 relates that the true meaning of the Scripture testifies to Jesus' fate in death and God's vindication of Jesus by raising him. Pilch notes that, "Such divinely inspired insight does not come from pouring over scrolls in search of answers. While that can help, ultimately God communicates the insight."[25]

Peter's vision in a waking dream is another instance of trance (Acts 10:9-16). This vision has been predicted by another ASC in which Cornelius sees an angelic visitor (Acts 10:1-8). Cornelius is told by the angel to send his people to retrieve Peter from Joppa (Acts 10:5). In the meantime, Peter "fell into a trance" (Acts 10:10). In this trance, Peter has a waking dream that includes various types of animals, both clean and unclean. The voice (of God) says, "Get up, Peter; kill and eat" (Acts 10:13). Peter initially refuses because he has made it his practice to eat only clean foods (foods deemed acceptable according to first-century CE understandings of the Pentateuch). The voice speaks to Peter twice more, "and the thing was suddenly taken up to heaven" (Acts 10:16). As in the case of Jesus' ascension, Peter is unclear as to the meaning of the vision. He receives further instruction when the Spirit alerts him to the presence of Cornelius' men approaching (Acts 10:17-23).

When Peter arrives at Cornelius' house, Cornelius bows down before Peter.[26] Peter, however, due to his status as a mortal, tells Cornelius to stand (Acts 10:25-26). Cornelius, like others in Acts (i.e., Acts 14:12), is unsure whether the status of the witnesses to the risen Christ is mortal or heavenly. It is in meeting Cornelius and hearing Cornelius' explanation of the vision that he saw that Peter comes to understand the full importance of his own waking dream (Acts 10:28-43). When Peter recognizes "that God shows no partiality" (Acts 10:34) and alerts the people to his witness concerning Jesus, the "Holy Spirit fell upon all who heard the word" (Acts 10:44). When the spirit comes upon them, the uncircumcised members of the Jesus movement have the same type of ASC experiences (i.e., speaking in tongues) as the disciples (Acts 10:46). The trance experiences that occur in the group are now occurring among initiates outside the context of the house of Israel, both in Cornelius and in those peoples (Gk: *ethnē*) who hear the word that Peter spoke.

Peter and the rest of the eleven practice a form of divination in Acts 1:16-26. Peter is aware of the meaning of Judas' death (Acts 1:16-20), and he suggests that they cast lots to determine his replacement (Acts 1:26). Both the knowledge of the meaning of Judas' fate in terms of Scripture and the casting of lots suggest that the disciples expected God to control the process and provide information regarding God's choice for the replacement of Judas. The prayer of the group (1:24) indicates an attempt to discover the answer to a question through access to the divine realm. Through both the practice of divination and the interpretation of Scripture, Peter (and the other disciples) performs one of the two functions of shamans: divination and education.

Peter also performs the other function of the shaman: healing and controlling spirits. Like Jesus in the Gospel of Luke, Peter heals people in Acts. Peter's first healing is narrated in Acts 3:1-10. There, Peter, together with John, heals a lame man. Pilch notes that the incident is rife with language that indicates an ASC experience. Much of this information comes in the power of the stare. Peter "looked intently" at the man and requests for the man to "look at us" (3:4). Staring intently at someone or something is one way to induce a trance or ASC experience.[27] Bruce Malina and John Pilch rightly note that this man is not "restored" since he had been "lame from birth" (Acts 3:2).[28] He is not restored but made whole, a condition in which he had not been since birth. Peter also heals another lame man, Aeneas (Acts 9:32-35), and restores Tabitha/Dorcas to life (9:36-42). The raising of Tabitha significantly parallels the raising of Jairus' daughter narrated in Luke 8:49-56. Most specifically, the command to "get up" (Luke 8:54; Acts 9:40) restores life to the daughter and to Tabitha. Like Jesus, Peter's word contains power to restore someone to life. It is interesting to note that of the three healings that Peter performs in Acts that are narrated, the raising of Tabitha is the only one in which Jesus' name is not invoked. Clearly,

Peter's ability to heal comes from God through Jesus via the Spirit. Even Peter's shadow is able to heal those upon whom it is cast (Acts 5:12-16). As possessor of the Spirit, he is able to heal through the power of the Spirit.[29]

Peter experiences a variety of ASCs in the book of Acts. He fulfills the roles of teaching and divining the will of Jesus (now a heavenly figure) and heals by his possession of the Spirit. As such, he is a holy person, brokering the benefactions of the God of Israel and his appointed agent, Jesus the Messiah (Acts 2:36). Through his reception of the Spirit at Pentecost, Peter is able to perform roles that were reserved for Jesus in the Gospel of Luke.

Peter as Moral Entrepreneur

In addition to being a holy person in the book of Acts, Peter is also a moral entrepreneur. A moral entrepreneur is an "individual, group, or formal organization that takes on the responsibility of persuading society to develop or enforce rules that are consistent with its own ardently held moral beliefs."[30] Moral entrepreneurship involves three main elements: rule making, rule enforcing, and rule interpreting.[31] Moral entrepreneurs can perform one or more of these tasks and do not have to perform all of them to fulfill the role of moral entrepreneur. In fact, it is common for these tasks to be performed by different people.

Moral entrepreneurs are those who label some persons, behaviors, or things as moral threats to society. When these labels stick, the persons, behaviors, or things in question come to be seen as deviant. Deviance is socially defined and "is inherent neither to a particular behavior nor to a particular rule breaker, but . . . is nothing more than a label successfully applied by more powerful entrepreneurs to rule violators."[32] Whether the label persuades others is a function of how compelling the moral entrepreneur's rhetoric is to those outside the movement.

Moral entrepreneurs are frequently founders of new movements or leaders of "revivals" of older movements. "The moral entrepreneur is the person likely to initiate a deviance process and to mobilize the forces necessary to make it successful."[33] If the moral entrepreneur is successful in labeling opponents as deviants, then he or she is usually able to create, enforce, and interpret rules for admission into or expulsion from the community. In the gospels, Jesus' focus on repentance and the forthcoming theocracy of the God of Israel makes Jesus a moral entrepreneur. Peter assumes this role in Acts.

Peter is the *de facto* leader of the group of disciples in the book of Acts. Peter "stood up" among the followers of Jesus (Acts 1:15) when he interpreted two psalms (1:20). This phrase is identical to the one used about Jesus when he "stood up" to read the Isaiah scroll in synagogue at Nazareth (Luke 4:16).[34] Peter establishes the procedure for securing a replacement for Judas (Acts 1:21-22).[35] Peter here performs the rule-making function of a moral entrepreneur.

When Jesus ascends, the two angels tell the disciples what has happened. Richard Pervo offers a meaning for this event by way of a parallel.[36] Noting that this account is modeled on the account of Elijah's ascension in 2 Kings 2:1-14, especially given that Elijah's ascent is the catalyst for the receipt of a double portion of Elijah's spirit, Pervo argues that the text in Acts 1:6-14 is a succession narrative. If this text is meant to suggest that Jesus is no longer the leader of the movement due to his relative inaccessibility, this might explain why the angels are present to tell the disciples that Jesus is now gone for an extended period (until the return of the Son of Man). Indeed, this text is to be the last time in the narrative of Acts that these disciples see Jesus.

Since the genesis of moral entrepreneurship is found in deviance theory, it is useful to note that Peter's behavior, as well as that of the other disciples, is regularly considered deviant in Acts. Peter and the other disciples are accused of being drunk (2:13); they are identified as companions of Jesus, a crucified criminal, by the high priest and others of priestly families (4:13); they arouse jealousy (5:17); and they cause people to want to kill them (5:33). Rather than accepting the claim that they are deviants, however, Peter routinely denies it and argues that those who stand in opposition to the disciples are the true deviants. Peter makes abundantly clear that the people as a whole, as well as the leaders of the aristocratic priestly families (4:10), are responsible for crucifying the Lord and Messiah (2:23, 36; 3:14-15). Peter's argument is precisely what one might expect from a moral entrepreneur. He appeals to traditions that are shared by his audience (the Scriptures of Israel), labeling his opponents' understanding of those Scriptures as deviant. Through his interpretation of Scripture, Peter performs the rule-interpretation function of a moral entrepreneur.

Acts portrays Peter as ultimately successful in this endeavor due to the large number of people who are persuaded to join the movement (Acts 2:41, 47; 4:4). Indeed, Peter's first speech to outsiders has the effect of causing the audience to be "cut to the heart" (2:37). Peter, as Jesus before him, tells the audience to repent, but here Peter adds that they are to be baptized in the name of Jesus in order to "receive the gift of the Holy Spirit" (2:38). After nearly three thousand were baptized, they "devoted themselves to the apostles' teaching and fellowship, to the breaking of bread and the prayers" (2:42). This scene shows Peter as both broker of the Spirit of God and as a moral entrepreneur. Peter is responsible in other cases for initiating large numbers of people into the movement as well (Acts 10:44), and, more significantly, he brokers the Spirit to those who join the movement. Besides Acts 10:44, Peter and John occasion the reception of the Spirit for the Samaritans when they lay their hands upon people who had joined the movement already (8:17). Not everyone who was baptized received the Spirit, which came "through the laying on of the apostles' hands" (8:18).

Peter performs the tasks of rule making when he decides how to replace Judas among the disciples (Acts 1:15-26). Moreover, Peter is the first to articulate how to make outsiders from the movement insiders (Acts 2:38). Nowhere are the disciples in Luke or Acts told to baptize new members to the movement, unlike in Matthew where such a task is ordered of the disciples after Jesus' resurrection. Peter is also responsible for rule enforcing when he is given the interpretation of his vision to allow non-Israelites into the community and not to forbid unclean foods (Acts 10:34-43) and, more problematically, in the case of Ananias and Sapphira (discussed more fully below). Finally, Peter also interprets the rule of the community at the council of Jerusalem (15:7-11) and in refusing to grant the Spirit to Simon Magus when he offers to pay for it (8:20-23).

Acts and Fictive Kinship

One of the more difficult texts to understand in Acts is the story of Ananias and Sapphira, found in Acts 5:1-11. This text is difficult because, due to lying, two of the members of the Jesus movement are killed, seemingly by God. This story must be understood within its context of the first six chapters of Acts. S. Scott Bartchy has argued that the description of the Jesus group in Acts 1–6 is that of a fictive family.[37] This group is fictive kin because of its adoption of kinship language to refer to one another, but even more because of their sharing of all of their possessions.[38] Relationships with non-family were characterized by two different types of reciprocity. Among those with whom one interacted on a daily basis (i.e., fellow villagers), one practiced balanced reciprocity. Balanced reciprocity consists of transactions in which one receives in equal measure to what one gives. Outside of this familiar context of daily interaction (i.e., with strangers), males were usually socialized to practice negative reciprocity. They were taught to try to gain more from the other party than they themselves had to give up. Within the context of kinship, however, generalized reciprocity was ideal. Generalized reciprocity is the exchange of goods, services, and other things of value (i.e., honor, potential mates, aid, or protection) without consideration of whether one came out ahead or behind. This type of reciprocity keeps no accounts, and it is the type that was practiced between husbands and wives or parents and children. It also, however, included siblings and their families.

The Jesus community in Jerusalem practiced generalized reciprocity. Three important notices point to this fact within Acts. These notices are the summary statements found in Acts 2:43-47; 4:32-37; and 5:12-16. These summaries of life within the community of Jerusalem stress the fact that these fictive kin shared their belongings without holding anything back from the group (2:45; 4:32, 35) and had access to healing (5:12-16). These descriptions, especially that "there was not a needy person among them" (4:32), describe the group as one living by the norm of generalized reciprocity expected among kin.

As in all groups in the first-century Mediterranean world, there are still status incongruities. Some people (i.e., the apostles [see Acts 5:13]) held statuses that were higher than others. Peter retains his position of leadership among the group even as they practice generalized reciprocity. Such status inconsistencies were part and parcel of all families in a patriarchal society. Another key element to note about fictive kinship arrangements is that family members are those to whom the truth is due.[39] Since the truth is not due to outsiders, "to lie really means to deny the truth to one who has the right to it."[40] Those who belong to the Jesus movement, living together in community as fictive kin, owe the truth to one another.

It is within this context of fictive kinship with its attendant obligations for both generalized reciprocity and truth telling that the story of Ananias and Sapphira should be understood.[41] The problem is that both Ananias and Sapphira lie to God (as Peter puts it), the heavenly patron and father of the fictive kin group. They neither participate in the generalized reciprocity described immediately beforehand (Acts 4:32-37) nor tell the truth to Peter and, by extension, God. Peter's word of accusation contains power and causes the death of Sapphira, at least (Acts 5:9), due to her deceitfulness toward the members of her fictive kin group. Peter's word, like Jesus' word (Luke 7:7; 24:19), carries with it power through the Spirit.

Peter's roles in Acts, as holy person and moral entrepreneur, go well beyond those roles he has in Paul's letters, the Synoptic Gospels, or in First Peter. Peter here adopts the social roles and a similar status to Jesus in the Gospel of Luke. Jesus' role there is summarized as a "prophet mighty in deed and word before God and all the people" (Luke 24:19). Peter's characterization in Acts, as the leader of the Jesus group and broker of the Spirit, makes him the mediator of God's favor in the same manner that Jesus mediates God's favor in Luke.

CHAPTER 5

Peter as the Author of Epistles

In addition to Peter as a first-generation proclaimer of the forthcoming theocracy, a change agent within the Jesus movement, a leader among the disciples, and a wonder-working broker of the Spirit, Peter is also remembered as a writer of letters. There are two letters attributed to Peter in the New Testament (1 Pet and 2 Pet), though most scholars agree that 2 Peter does not come from Peter. As early as the fourth century CE, Eusebius, the famous historian of early Christianity, had questions about the authorship of these two letters attributed to Peter. Eusebius treats the matter in his *Ecclesiastical History* 3.3.1–7. He firmly states in discussing the numerous materials ascribed to Peter by various authors of the first-, second-, and third-century Jesus movement that "among the works named for Peter, I know only one legitimate letter and such things are agreed among the ancient presbyters."[1] Eusebius cites elders of the church to support his argument that 2 Peter was not written by Peter.

Pseudonymity, writing in the name of another person, was a common practice in the Roman period. The author of 2 Peter attempted to invoke the "voice" of Peter to lend authority to his claims. Pseudonymity, for the most part, was not considered morally objectionable in antiquity.² The author of 2 Peter, for example, invoked Peter's name to lend support to ideas and exhortations that he or she assumed Peter would have shared, had Peter been present (or alive) to write concerning the same matters.

Assessing whether 1 Peter is a pseudonymous letter is more difficult. There are several reasons to think that it was not written by Peter. Foremost among these reasons is the description of Peter as "illiterate" (Acts 4:13). Of course, if Peter were illiterate, he could not have composed this letter. Writing in antiquity, however, frequently involved the employment of scribes or secretaries to whom one could dictate a letter. For this reason, even if Peter himself were illiterate, it would not rule out Peter as the source of the material contained in 1 Peter. There are a number of factors, however, that make it unlikely that Peter dictated the letter to a scribe who wrote it.³ The style and the vocabulary of the Greek are quite sophisticated and are not likely the words of a Galilean fisherman. As a fisherman, it is unlikely that Peter had any formal education. Furthermore, during Peter's lifetime, there were several languages into which the writings that became the Hebrew Bible/Old Testament were translated. Peter and his companions spoke Aramaic, the common language of Galilee during the first century CE. The biblical citations in 1 Peter come from the Septuagint (the Greek translation of the Hebrew Scriptures) rather than from the Hebrew (Masoretic) text or from the Aramaic Targums (translated and expanded versions of Hebrew texts). It is unlikely that an Aramaic speaker would cite Greek texts rather than Aramaic or perhaps Hebrew texts. First Peter also contains virtually nothing concerning the words, life, or ministry of Jesus. If Peter were its author, we would expect to hear something about his time spent with Jesus. Finally, there is "no historical evidence that Peter himself missionized in Asia Minor, and 1 Peter contains no mention of any direct personal contact between Peter and the addressees."⁴ The areas to which the text is sent are not areas to which Peter ever traveled. In addition to these factors, the major concern of the first-generation members of the Jesus group, the kingdom/reign of God, is absent from the letter.

A man named Silvanus is mentioned in 1 Peter 5:12. There the author says "Through Silvanus, whom I consider a faithful brother, I have written this short letter to encourage you and to testify that this is the true grace of God." Some scholars have suggested that Silvanus might be the author of the letter, but John H. Elliott argues that this phrase refers to a carrier of a letter rather than its author: "Silvanus is identified and commended . . . as the letter's *courier*, not its drafter."[5] Elliott concludes that "it is virtually certain that 1 Peter is a pseudonymous letter ascribed to the Apostle Peter and produced not by Silvanus but either by someone remaining anonymous or by some group to which reference in the letter is made."[6] Neither 1 Peter nor 2 Peter, then, were written by Peter the disciple of Jesus.

Among the more interesting considerations among scholars regarding 1 Peter is the question of its relationship to the Pauline letters. That Paul adopted this format rather than others for communicating with the communities that he founded (and at least one that he did not in Rome) gives license to modern interpreters to assume that those within Pauline circles considered letters a significant form of communication. The very fact that at least some of Paul's letters are preserved and were then circulated more widely than among the cities to which they were originally sent evinces some significant interest in Paul's letters.

Toward the end of the first century, Paul's letters began to circulate as a collection. Numerous other early leaders of the Jesus movement also wrote letters toward the end of the first century (most notably, Polycarp). The attribution of letters to Peter has caused scholars to wonder whether these letters could have been written by coworkers of Paul. There are several elements in 1 Peter that bear resemblance to Paul's letters and thought. David G. Horrell discusses several of these "Pauline" elements of the letter.[7] In the framing of 1 Peter, noticeable elements seemingly borrowed from Paul's letters include the description of Peter as "apostle of Jesus Christ" (1:1), the greeting of "grace and peace" (1:2), and the mention of the kiss (5:14). First Peter refers to the kiss as "of love" rather than "holy," as Paul refers to it.[8] First Peter also uses significant terms found elsewhere in the New Testament only in Paul's letters: "in Christ" (1 Pet 3:16; 5:10; 5:14), charisma as a description of gifts of the Spirit (1 Pet 4:10), and the concept of no longer conforming to older patterns (1 Pet 1:14).[9] There are also similarities between the injunction not to return evil for evil in Romans 12:17; 1 Thessalonians 5:15; and 1 Peter 3:9.[10]

Despite these similarities to the Pauline letters, there are several elements that distinguish 1 Peter from Paul's letters and thought.[11] Outside of 1 Peter 1:1, the use of the term "Dispersion" (Gk: *Diaspora*) is found elsewhere in the New Testament only in John 7:35 and James 1:1. This term refers to those Israelites (descendants of the twelve tribes) not living within the land of Judea. First Peter also alludes to a number of traditions found in the Synoptic Gospels, frequently those found in Matthew. The letter contains numerous christological elements that draw on Isaiah 53, especially focusing on Christ as the pure lamb whose blood was shed (1 Pet 1:19). The christological creeds of 1 Peter (1:18-21; 2:21-25; 3:18-22) "while paralleled to some extent in the Pauline corpus (cf. esp. 1 Tim. 3:16; 2 Tim. 1:9-10; Titus 2:14), do not represent specifically Pauline formulas."[12]

Elliott has argued that 1 Peter is the product of a Petrine circle in Rome rather than a letter in the Pauline tradition.[13] He argues for the existence of a Petrine circle in Rome from basically two different angles. He asserts that it is likely that Peter, like Paul and other missionaries, worked with groups of people rather than alone.[14] Given what is known about early missionary efforts in the first-century Jesus movement, Elliott's case is certainly more probable than its alternative. As we saw in chapter 2, Peter's social network was active in Corinth even as Peter himself did not travel there. Second, Elliott argues that the "explicit naming of Silvanus and Mark in 1 Pet 5:12-13 makes sense if they were actually intimate colleagues of the Apostle Peter and associated with the composition and dispatch of the letter in Peter's name."[15] These associates of Peter are "friends" of Peter in network terms that carry his message forward. It is clear in Elliott's arguments, taken together with those of Horrell, that describing 1 Peter as a "Pauline" document without qualification will not do.

The question remains, however, what this letter might tell us about portraits of Peter in the last quarter of the first century CE. We have no direct knowledge of a circle of Peter's associates in Rome in the last years of the first century. Horrell notes two difficulties with Elliott's arguments regarding a Petrine circle. The first difficulty relates to the identification of Silvanus and Mark. Silvanus is frequently identified with the Silas of Acts.[16] Perhaps due to this identification, and especially when it is combined with the report of Papias linking Mark to Peter as his "secretary," the Mark mentioned in 1 Peter is often identified as the John Mark of Acts. Acts does, in fact, link both Silvanus/Silas and Mark to Peter, but not in an especially strong way. Horrell argues that the evidence from Acts concerning "Silvanus and Mark would suggest that their links were both with Peter/Jerusalem and with Paul."[17] In the case of Acts, moreover, the link between Silvanus/Silas and Paul is stronger than the link to Peter. For Peter, Silvanus delivers a letter together with Barnabas, and they travel together with Paul (Acts 15:25). Silvanus/Silas is identified as a traveling companion of Paul throughout much of the central section of the narrative of Acts (15:40–18:5).[18] Moreover, Silvanus is listed with Timothy as a traveling companion of Paul in Paul's letters (2 Cor 1:19; 1 Thess 1:1; 2 Thess 2:2). Relating (John) Mark to Peter is even more tenuous. The only evidence in Acts that links Peter to Mark is that Peter visited Mark's mother's house (Acts 12:12) when Mark was away. The fact that the author of 1 Peter calls Mark "my son" (1 Pet 5:13) indicates a close relationship between the two, and the fact that Mark's mother's house is located in Jerusalem in Acts could suggest a substantial amount of contact between the two, but what the traveling Mark does as a missionary is related to Paul rather than to Peter. The evidence in Acts does not seem to indicate that Silvanus/Silas and (John) Mark were particularly close associates of Peter.

A further difficulty with suggesting that 1 Peter is the product of a specifically Petrine circle is, as Horrell argues, that it is much more likely that 1 Peter represents "both Jewish-Christian (Jerusalem) and Pauline traditions."[19] The letter looks much more like a fourth-generation document than it does a first-generation document. "As such, 1 Peter does not appear to be the product of a Petrine circle, nor indeed of a Pauline circle, but rather of a Roman Christianity in which diverse and sometimes opposing Christian traditions were drawn together."[20] This understanding of Peter as one who draws together both Messianic Jesus groups and Risen Christ groups is much more in line with the image of Peter that we find in Acts.

Peter is a figure who is appropriated in numerous ways by many people claiming his legacy. His stature as a figure of authority seemed to grow throughout the first centuries of the Jesus movement.[21] Horrell suggests that perhaps Peter is employed in this document because of Paul's lack of success in the areas to which it was addressed, Paul's contested legacy, and the fact that Paul's letters "were soon seen as dangerously open to diverse interpretations."[22] Peter's stature and the difficulties with invoking Paul's name provide sufficient reason for attributing the letter to Peter rather than to Paul or some other figure in the early Jesus movement.

If it is correct to assume that this document is the product of a late first-century Roman Jesus group, what does their choice to invoke Peter's name say about Peter? In the first case, it says that Peter was a known and respected leader in the Jesus movement in Rome. The author(s) of the letter presumably also thought invoking his authorial presence would persuade those to whom the letter was sent. This portrayal of Peter resembles the one found in Acts in a variety of ways. If Horrell is correct that the letter is an amalgamation of numerous ideas of the Jesus movement, then Peter as the representative of such an amalgamation fits nicely with the picture of Peter in Acts. The letter addresses both Judeans and non-Judeans, Peter is the leader of the leaders of the community, and he is witness to the sufferings of Christ.

All of these elements cohere very well with the portrait of Peter in Acts. The tensions between Peter and Paul in the middle of the first century around questions of *halakhic* observance have given way to the apostles as sub-brokers of the benefits of God, which they have received from the resurrected Jesus. The borrowings from the epistolary structure of Paul's letters in 1 Peter further demonstrate the common nature of their endeavor.

CONCLUSION

Descriptions of the personage "Peter" within the New Testament show some significant variation. All of the characterizations of Peter link him to the earliest stages of Jesus' movement. He was a proclaimer of the kingdom of God, recruited to the movement by Jesus himself. When Jesus died, Peter and the other disciples experienced the risen Jesus and altered their message to include a soon-to-return Jesus who would inaugurate the forthcoming theocracy. These first-generation groups continued to observe *halakhic* practices as Jesus had taught them to do. They also attempted to persuade others to join the Jesus Messiah movement and to recognize Jesus as the anointed agent of the God of Israel who would soon return to judge the people of Israel.

The portrait of Peter in the second-generation New Testament documents, Galatians and 1 Corinthians, shows some tension between Peter and Paul and indicates the separate (though related) nature of their missions. Peter, representing first-generation concerns, focuses on the message of God's kingdom to the members of Israel. Paul, representing second-generation concerns, focuses on the work of God in the death and resurrection of Jesus and the cosmic implications of what had occurred. Furthermore, Paul was a member of the Risen Christ movement, which did not focus on the maintenance of *halakhic* practices or the exclusion of the *ethnē* from the movement. Since we do not have any account of these encounters from Peter, nor from any other first-generation source, we are limited to an understanding of Peter provided by a second-generation writer who did not consider the performance of *halakhic* practices necessary for uncircumcised members of the Jesus movement.

The gospels "remember" Peter in slightly varying ways. In Mark, Peter is foremost among the disciples, but he lacks fidelity to Jesus at key moments. Matthew retains this characterization of Peter, though it amplifies his role as one lacking faithfulness (Matt 14:31), while at the same time elevating Peter's role among the disciples (Matt 16:18-19; 18:21-22). Luke omits from his story most of the accounts of Peter's lack of fidelity, retaining only Peter's denials. These denials, however, are identified by Jesus as a result of the power of Satan (Luke 22:31), and Peter is identified as the disciple who will reconstitute the group after Jesus' death (Luke 22:32).

By the end of the first century and into the second century, portrayals of Peter focused on his role as the leader of a universal movement in harmony with Paul. Acts erases the distinction between Peter and Paul by claiming that it is Peter who is the one by whom the gospel would be preached among the Gentiles (Acts 15:7). Peter is given a divine revelation that instructs him not to distinguish between clean and unclean foods (Acts 11:9-10). This designation explicitly contradicts the earlier description of the agreement between the leaders of the Jerusalem community and Paul in Galatians 2. Furthermore, Peter is the reputed author of a letter that seeks to bridge the divide between Judean and non-Judean members of the Jesus movement.

Peter's characterization continued to develop long after the composition of the texts found in the New Testament. By the third century, the Acts of Peter suggest that Peter traveled to Rome in order to substitute there for Paul, who had traveled to Spain. In this text, Peter is the champion of the local populace of Jesus followers and wins a miracle competition against Simon Magus. All of the followers of Jesus in this third-century text are non-Judean, and Peter's concern for Judean Jesus followers is nowhere present in this story. He has fully accepted the admission of non-Judeans into the movement and does not accept those who maintain *halakhic* practices any longer. The beginning of this "inclusive" Peter is found in the Gospels of Mark and Luke, where the distinction between Judeans and the *ethnē* began to be dismissed. By the fourth generation, Peter is a champion of admitting the *ethnē* into the Jesus movement. This characterization of Peter becomes the dominant one into the second and third centuries, where Peter and Paul together were considered the first apostles of the church at Rome and the founders of that church.

Each generation of the Jesus movement remembered Peter differently. The reason for his significance in the movement was his association with Jesus. The third generation remembered the relationship between the historical person Jesus and Peter, while the second and fourth generations highlighted the appearances of the risen Christ to Peter. For the first and third generations, Peter held a unique place in the Jesus movement as an early adopter of Jesus' proclamation of the kingdom of God. For the second and fourth generations, although Peter held a place of honor, his access to both the heavenly Christ and his possession of the Spirit distinguished him from some, though not all, followers of Jesus. Access to the heavenly Christ was available to followers outside the circle of Jesus' earthly companions, and possession of the Spirit, at least by the fourth generation, was widely available through the brokerage of those who already possessed it.

The remembrance of Peter was modified as the needs of the communities of Jesus' followers developed and changed. Peter's characterization was quite malleable in the first three centuries of the Jesus movement. This malleability, taken together with his relationship to the historical person Jesus, allowed for Peter's influence to cast a very long shadow over the early church. These two followers of Jesus, Peter and Paul, are the most widely remembered and claimed personages of the early Jesus movement.

NOTES

Notes to Introduction (pages 1–8)

1. For a recent attempt to do such historical reconstruction and to disentangle "myth" from "history," see Bart D. Ehrman, *Peter, Paul, and Mary Magdalene: The Followers of Jesus in History and Legend* (Oxford: Oxford University Press, 2006), 3–86. See also John P. Meier, *A Marginal Jew: Rethinking the Historical Jesus*, vol. 3: *Companions and Competitors* (New York: Doubleday, 2001), 221–45.

2. For a recent discussion of Peter's treatment in the four canonical gospels, see Richard J. Cassidy, *Four Times Peter: Portrayals of Peter in the Four Gospels and at Philippi*, Interfaces (Collegeville, MN: Liturgical Press, 2007).

3. For an introduction, discussion, and analysis of these types of approaches, see John H. Elliott, *What Is Social-Scientific Criticism?*, Guides to Biblical Scholarship (Minneapolis: Fortress, 1993).

4. Harry C. Triandis, *Individualism and Collectivism*, New Directions in Social Psychology (Boulder, CO: Westview, 1995), 2.

5. Ibid., 2.

6. This chart is loosely adapted from Bruce J. Malina and Jerome H. Neyrey, *Portraits of Paul: An Archaeology of Ancient Personality* (Louisville, KY: Westminster John Knox, 1996), 227–31.

7. Krister Stendahl, "Paul and the Introspective Conscience of the West," *HTR* 56 (1963): 206.

8. Ibid., 214. See also Bruce J. Malina, "Rhetorical Criticism and Social-Scientific Criticism: Why Won't Romanticism Leave us Alone?," in *The Social World of the New Testament: Insights and Models*, ed. Jerome H. Neyrey and Eric C. Stewart (Peabody, MA: Hendrickson, 2008), 5–21.

9. Malina and Neyrey, *Portraits of Paul*, 3–4.

10. See Jerome H. Neyrey, "The Social Location of Paul: Education as the Key," in *Fabrics of Discourse: Essays in Honor of Vernon K. Robbins*, ed. David B. Gowler et al. (Harrisburg, PA: Trinity Press International, 2003), 126–64.

11. Of course, there is information regarding his mother-in-law in Mark 1:29-31 and parallels. We must presume that this relationship means he had a wife at some point. As we shall see below, Paul seems to indicate the same for Peter (1 Cor 9:5). Peter also seems to be engaged in the family business, indicated by the presence of his brother in the boat with him in the Markan and Matthean versions of the story (Mark 1:16-17 // Matt 4:18-19), though he is absent in the parallel account in Luke. In a patrilineal and patriarchal society, however, the lack of information regarding Peter's father's family (or even Peter's tribe) is remarkable. It might be assumed that his father had died before Jesus' arrival alongside the sea, given that the father of James and John is mentioned (Mark 1:20).

Notes to Chapter 1 (pages 9–15)

1. On this point, see John P. Meier, *A Marginal Jew: Rethinking the Historical Jesus*, vol. 3: *Companions and Competitors* (New York: Doubleday, 2001), 222.

2. Bruce J. Malina, "From the Jesus Faction to the Synoptic Gospels: The Synoptic Gospels as Third Generation Phenomenon," in *Kontexte der Schrift Band II: Kultur, Politik, Sprache-Text: Wolfgang Stegemann zum 60. Geburtstag*, ed. Chrisian Strecker (Stuttgart, Ger.: Kohlhammer, 2005), 61–74.

3. Marcus Lee Hansen, *The Problem of the Third Generation Immigrant: A Reproduction of the 1937 Address with Introductions by Peter Kivisto and Oscar Handlin* (Rock Island, IL: Swenson Swedish Immigration Research Center, 1987).

4. Malina, "From the Jesus Faction," 62.

5. Ibid., 63.

6. Ibid., 64.

7. Ibid., 65.

8. Bruce J. Malina, *The Social Gospel of Jesus: The Kingdom of God in Mediterranean Perspective* (Minneapolis: Fortress, 2001), 117.

9. Ibid., 153–57.

10. Malina, "From the Jesus Faction," 63.

11. Ibid., 66–69. According to Hansen, *Problem of the Third Generation Immigrant*, such selective forgetting is part of a regular pattern from first-generation to second-generation groups after traumatic events. Hansen discusses specifically geographic displacement through migration in his book, but he argues that his test cases in American immigration point to a broader pattern throughout history (15–17).

12. Malina, "From the Jesus Faction," 66–67.

13. Ibid., 67. Possible tensions between the first- and second-generation Jesus groups will be examined in more detail in chapter 2.

14. Ibid., 67.

15. Hansen, *Problem of the Third Generation Immigrant*, 15–17.

16. For more on this point, see chapter 3. See also Ritva H. Williams, *Stewards, Prophets, Keepers of the Word: Leadership in the Early Church* (Peabody, MA: Hendrickson, 2006), 146–83.

17. The chart is based on Malina, "From the Jesus Faction."

Notes to Chapter 2 (pages 16–29)

1. Much of the following discussion is based on the work of Jeremy Boissevain, *Friends of Friends: Networks, Manipulators, Coalitions* (Oxford: Basil Blackwell, 1974).

2. Ibid., 27.

3. Ibid., 30

4. Ibid., 33.

5. Ibid.

6. Ibid., 34.

7. This statement, of course, does not rule out the possibility that they saw each other more than the three occasions mentioned in Galatians. What is significant here, however, is that Paul does not discuss any more direct encounters between them in his letters.

8. Bruce J. Malina, "From the Jesus Faction to the Synoptic Gospels: The Synoptic Gospels as Third Generation Phenomenon," in *Kontexte der Schrift Band II: Kultur, Politik, Sprache-Text: Wolfgang Stegemann zum 60. Geburtstag*, ed. Chrisian Strecker (Stuttgart, Ger.: Kohlhammer, 2005), 66–67.

9. Ibid., 67.

10. For more on what it means to "see" the resurrected Jesus, see the discussion about altered-states-of-consciousness experiences in chapter four.

11. The following discussion is based in large part on Everett M. Rogers, *Diffusion of Innovations*, 5th ed. (New York: Free Press, 2003), 365–401.

12. We might consider, as an example, what it means to be "friends" with someone on Facebook. Some Facebook friends know one another quite well, while others have never met in person. Facebook friends may have a variety of role relations with one another, and they may not necessarily be equals in the roles they play. Nonetheless, within the social network of Facebook, they are "friends."

13. Richard L. Rohrbaugh, "Honor: Core Value in the Biblical World," in, *Understanding the Social World of the New Testament*, eds. Dietmar Neufeld and Richard E. DeMaris (London: Routledge, 2010), 109–125.

14. Craig S. Keener, "The Pillars and the Right Hand of Fellowship in Galatians 2:9," in *Journal of Greco-Roman Christianity and Judaism* 7 (2010): 54.

15. Ibid., 54.

16. See Joseph H. Hellerman, *The Ancient Church as Family* (Minneapolis: Fortress, 2001), 92–167.

17. Bruce J. Malina, *The Social Gospel of Jesus: The Kingdom of God in Mediterranean Perspective* (Minneapolis: Fortress, 2001), 158.

18. This discussion is based on Ibid., 141–161.

19. Ibid., 156.

20. Ibid., 159.

Notes to Chapter 3 (pages 30–51)

1. See Marcus Lee Hansen, *The Problem of the Third-Generation Immigrant: A Reproduction of the 1937 Address with Introductions by Peter Kivisto and Oscar Handlin* (Rock Island, IL: Swenson Swedish Immigration Research Center, 1987); and Bruce J. Malina, "From the Jesus Faction to the Synoptic Gospels: The Synoptic Gospels as Third-Generation Phenomenon," in *Kontexte der Schrift Band II: Kultur, Politik, Sprache-Text: Wolfgang Stegemann zum 60. Geburtstag*, ed. Chrisian Strecker (Stuttgart, Ger.: Kohlhammer, 2005).

2. Bruce J. Malina, *Timothy: Paul's Closest Associate*, Paul's Social Network: Brothers and Sisters in Faith (Collegeville, MN: Michael Glazier, 2008), 41.

3. Two of the clearest examples of this redefining of the ingroup and outgroup are found in Mark 7:24-30, in which Jesus heals a Syrophonecian woman's daughter, and the healing of the Roman centurion's slave in Matthew 8:5-13//Luke 7:1-10.

4. For a discussion of the Synoptic Problem, see John S. Kloppenborg, *Excavating Q: The History and Setting of the Sayings Gospel* (Edinburgh: T & T Clark, 2000), 11–54.

5. For Q as it has been reconstructed by the International Q Project, see James M. Robinson et al., *The Critical Edition of Q*, Hermeneia (Minneapolis: Fortress, 2000).

6. James Robinson, *Jesus according to the Earliest Witnesses* (Minneapolis: Fortress, 2007), 239.

7. Ibid.

8. Ibid., 240. Robinson notes, however, that the final editing of Q was likely done in the aftermath of the Jewish War. So even here the "fit" with the first generation is not perfect.

9. Malina, "From the Jesus Faction," 64–65.

10. Ibid., 64.

11. Q is typically numbered according to its Lukan parallels. Q 10:5-9, then, is equivalent to Luke 10:5-9 and Matthew 20:7, 10b, 12-14.

12. See Jeffrey K. Olick, "Collective Memory: The Two Cultures," *Sociological Theory* 17, no. 3 (1999): 333–48.

13. Ibid., 335.

14. Jeffrey K. Olick and Joyce Robbins, "Social Memory Studies: From 'Collective Memory' to the Sociology of Mnemonic Practices," *Annual Review of Sociology* 24 (1998): 105–40.

15. For a useful discussion of this difference, see David A. Sánchez, *From Patmos to the Barrio: Subverting Imperial Myths* (Minneapolis: Fortress, 2008).

16. For one example of how such social memory processes worked in the first century of the Jesus movement, see Ritva H. Williams, "Social Memory and the Didachē," *BTB* 36 (2006): 35–39. See also Ritva Williams, *Stewarts, Prophets, Keepers of the Word: Leadership in the Early Church* (Peabody, MA: Hendrickson, 2006), 137–83.

17. Malina, *Timothy*, 41.

18. See Malina and Pilch, *Social-Science Commentary on the Letters of Paul* (Minneapolis: Fortress, 2006), 392–93.

19. For an understanding of the economy of first-century CE Galilee, see K. C. Hanson and Douglas E. Oakman, *Palestine in the Time of Jesus: Social Structures and Social Conflicts*, 2nd ed. (Minneapolis: Fortress, 2008), 93–122.

20. On the following, see the work of K. C. Hanson, "The Galilean Fishing Economy and the Jesus Tradition," *Biblical Theology Bulletin* 27 (1997): 99–111.

21. Ibid., 105.

22. Ibid.

23. Bruce J. Malina and Richard L. Rohrbaugh, *Social-Science Commentary on the Gospel of John* (Minneapolis: Fortress, 1998), 55. See also Zeba A. Crook, *Reconceptualising Conversion: Patronage, Loyalty, and Conversion in the Religions of the Ancient Mediterranean* (Berlin: de Gruyter, 2004), 230–31.

24. Bruce J. Malina, *Timothy*, 29.

25. Richard L. Rohrbaugh, "Ethnocentrism and Historical Questions about Jesus," in *The Social Setting of Jesus and the Gospels*, ed. Wolfgang Stegemann et al. (Minneapolis: Fortress, 2002), 27–43.

26. Here the language is borrowed from Zechariah 13:7.

27. See Bruce J. Malina and Jerome H. Neyrey, *Portraits of Paul: An Archaeology of Ancient Personality* (Louisville, KY: Westminster John Knox, 1996). Also, Eric C. Stewart, *Gathered around Jesus: An Alternative Spatial Practice in the Gospel of Mark* (Eugene, OR: Cascade, 2009).

28. Peter swears an oath twice in the Matthean text as opposed to once in the Markan text, there are two different slave girls in the Matthean text as opposed to one in the Markan text, and the cock crows only once in the Matthean version.

29. This text, of course, has been the focus of intense scrutiny among Catholic and Protestant theologians because of the authority seemingly granted to Peter in this passage. It is beyond the scope of this book to treat such matters extensively, but see Pheme Perkins, *Peter: Apostle for the Whole Church*, Studies of the Personalities of the New Testament (Columbia: University of South Carolina Press), 3–14, for such discussion.

30. Bruce J. Malina and Richard L. Rohrbaugh, *Social-Science Commentary on the Synoptic Gospels*, 2nd ed. (Minneapolis: Fortress, 2003), 87.

31. Perkins, *Peter*, 67.

32. Ibid.

33. Hanson, "Galilean Fishing Economy," 105.

34. Malina and Rohrbaugh, *Social-Science Commentary on the Synoptic Gospels*, 245.

35. John S. Kloppenborg ("'Exitus clari viri': The Death of Jesus in Luke," *Toronto Journal of Theology* 8, no. 1 [1992]: 106–20) and Gregory Sterling ("*Mors philosophi*: The Death of Jesus in Luke," *Harvard Theological Review* 94, no. 4 [2001]: 383–402) argue that Luke "cleans up" the image of Jesus in the passion narrative by setting his death within the tradition of "noble death." Perhaps it is not surprising, then, to see Peter as also a character whose weaknesses are downplayed somewhat.

36. In addition to the material that follows, Peter, together with John, is given the task of preparing the Passover meal (Luke 22:8).

37. See Raymond E. Brown, *The Community of the Beloved Disciple: The Life, Loves, and Hates of an Individual Church in New Testament Times* (New York: Paulist Press, 1979), 84–87.

Notes to Chapter 4 (pages 52–66)

1. The NSRV reads "brothers" (Gk: *adelphoi*) in Luke 22:32. This gender-exclusive reading is quite probably predicated upon those present with Jesus at the last meal with the disciples. Luke relates that Jesus "took his

place at the table, and the apostles with him" (Luke 22:14). Since there are apparently no females present at the meal in Luke's telling, the literal translation "brothers" fits the context. If, however, one agrees with the majority scholarly opinion that Luke and Acts are two volumes of the same work, the word might be more correctly translated "siblings" given the audience in Jerusalem of the reconstituted Jesus group. There are men and women among the early community in Jerusalem according to Luke's account in Acts (Acts 1:14).

2. *Parrēsia* is a key mark of distinction between flatterers and friends. Discussion of the idea of such frank speech is common among philosophers. See especially Plutarch, "How to Tell a Flatterer from a Friend."

3. G. William Farthing, *The Psychology of Consciousness* (Englewood Cliffs, NJ: Prentice Hall, 1992), 205.

4. Bruce J. Malina and John J. Pilch, *Social-Science Commentary on the Book of Acts* (Minneapolis: Fortress, 2008), 67.

5. John J. Pilch, *Visions and Healing in the Acts of the Apostles: How Early Believers Experienced God* (Collegeville, MN: Liturgical Press, 2004), 17–18.

6. Jean Clottes and David Lewis-Williams, *The Shamans of Prehistory: Trance and Magic in the Painted Caves*, trans. Sophie Hawkes (New York: Harry N. Abrams, Inc., 1998), 13.

7. Malina and Pilch, *Social-Science Commentary on the Book of Acts*, 185.

8. Pieter Craffert, "Shamanism and the Shamanic Complex," *Biblical Theology Bulletin* 41, no.3 (2011): 151–61.

9. Ibid., 156.

10. Pilch, *Visions and Healing*, 5. Those people who experience ASCs, other than those socially "acceptable" ASCs like drunkenness or dreams, are frequently treated as mentally ill in modern Western cultures like the United States.

11. See Gregory J. Riley, *One Jesus, Many Christs: How Jesus Inspired Not One True Christianity, But Many; The Truth about Christian Origins* (San Francisco: HarperSanFrancisco, 1997), 31–96. See also Pilch, *Visions and Healing*, 3.

12. Craffert, "Shamanism," 153.

13. Pilch, *Visions and Healing*, 4.

14. Ibid.

15. It is worth noting, of course, that these terms are etic rather than emic terms. Emic terms are those that occur within the culture group itself. Etic terms are used by theorists and those outside the group to describe the behaviors of group members. These etic terms come from the work of anthropologists and psychiatrists. For an examination of these same phenomena employing emic terms, see Riley, *One Jesus, Many Christs*.

16. John J. Pilch, *Stephen: Paul and the Hellenist Israelites*, Paul's Social Network: Brothers and Sisters in Faith (Collegeville, MN: Michael Glazier, 2004), 52.

17. In terms of type of ASC, these visions of the risen Jesus by the disciples gathered in Jerusalem are of the same type as the ASC experience of Paul in Acts 9.

18. Clottes and Lewis-Williams, *Shamans of Prehistory*, 14, admit that trance is "another word that is hard to define."

19. Ibid. On the resurrection accounts as ASC visions, see Pieter Craffert, "'I "Witnessed" the Raising of the Dead': Resurrection Accounts in a Neuro-anthropological Perspective," *Neotestamentica* 45, no. 1 (2011): 1–28.

20. Malina and Pilch, *Social-Science Commentary on the Book of Acts*, 185.

21. Pilch, *Visions and Healing*, 14–22.

22. Ibid., 21.

23. Felicitas D. Goodman, *Ecstasy, Ritual, and Alternate Reality: Religion in a Pluralistic World* (Bloomington: Indiana University Press, 1988), 47–48, 106–34.

24. Ibid, 48.

25. Pilch, *Visions and Healing*, 35.

26. The NRSV reads "worshiped him," but the literal meaning of the Greek term is to "do obeisance" or "bow down."

27. Pilch, *Visions and Healing*, 41.

28. Malina and Pilch, *Social-Science Commentary on the Book of Acts*, 38.

29. Possession of the Spirit does not always work to the benefit of those with whom Peter interacts. The power of Peter's word causes the death of Ananias and Sapphira in Acts 5:1-11.

30. Mary de Young, "Moral Entrepreneur," in *The Blackwell Encyclopedia of Sociology*, ed. George Ritzer (Malden, MA: Blackwell, 2007), 6:3086.

31. Ibid.

32. Ibid., 3087.

33. Malina and Pilch, *Social-Science Commentary on the Book of Acts*, 222.

34. In Luke 4:16 the Greek verb is the aorist active indicative form of the Greek verb *anistêmi* while in Acts 1:15 it is the aorist participle of the same verb. In both cases it means "to rise or stand up," and it is indicative of assuming a position of authority in these cases.

35. It is certainly a curiosity that the author of Acts relays the story of the choosing of Matthias to reconstitute the Twelve and then does not mention the Twelve as twelve again in the narrative. See Richard I. Pervo, *Acts*, Hermeneia (Minneapolis: Fortress, 2009), 49.

36. Ibid., 45–46.

37. S. Scott Bartchy, "Divine Power, Community Formation, and Leadership in the Acts of the Apostles," in *Community Formation in the Early Church*

and in the Church Today, ed. Richard N. Longenecker (Peabody, MA: Hendrickson, 2002), 89–104.

38. Bartchy, "Divine Power," 93–95. For more on the concept of generalized reciprocity, see Eric C. Stewart, "Social Stratification and Patronage," in *Understanding the Social World of the New Testament*, ed. Dietmar Neufeld and Richard E. DeMaris (London: Routledge, 2010), 160–70. See also Bruce J. Malina, *The New Testament World: Insights from Cultural Anthropology*, 3rd ed. (Louisville, KY: Westminster John Knox, 2001), 94–95.

39. See Bartchy, "Divine Power," 94.

40. Malina, *New Testament World*, 42.

41. So also Bartchy, "Divine Power," 94.

Notes to Chapter 5 (pages 67–73)

1. Translation is my own.

2. John H. Elliott, *1 Peter: A New Translation with Introduction and Commentary*, Anchor Bible 37B (New York: Doubleday, 2000), 118–20.

3. On what follows, see ibid., 121–125.

4. Ibid., 120. Other factors that Elliott notes mitigate against Petrine authorship include the indications that the letter was written after 70 CE while virtually all writers of the second century share the tradition that Peter was martyred in 64 CE in Rome under Nero, that no one before Iraneaus (*Haer.* 4.9.2) spoke of Peter as the letter's author, and that Peter is referred to as "co-elder," a title nowhere else ascribed to him in the New Testament (120–21).

5. Ibid., 124.

6. Ibid., 124–25.

7. David G. Horrell, "The Product of a Petrine Circle? A Reassessment of the Origin and Character of 1 Peter," *JSNT* 86 (2002): 29–60.

8. Ibid., 33. Paul refers to the holy kiss in Romans 16:16; 1 Corinthians 16:20; 2 Corinthians 13:12; and 1 Thessalonians 5:26.

9. Ibid., 33–37. The Greek word for no longer conforming to older patterns is *suschêmatizô* and is found in the New Testament only in 1 Peter 1:14 and Romans 12:2.

10. Horrell (ibid., 35) notes that this injunction is found also in the sermon on the Mount/Plain in Matthew 5:44 and Luke 6:27-28. He concludes that it is neither specifically Pauline nor Petrine but comes instead from "a common source in early Christian (dominical) paraenesis." There are significant linguistic parallels among the texts in Romans, 1 Thessalonians, and 1 Peter, however, that are not shared by the Synoptic tradition (the Greek verb *apodidômi* and the Greek phrase *kakon anti kakou*).

11. Ibid., 38–42.

12. Ibid., 41.

13. Ellliott, *1 Peter*, 127–29. See also John H. Elliott, *Conflict, Community, and Honor: 1 Peter in Social-Scientific Perspective*, Cascade Companions (Eugene: Cascade, 2007).

14. Ibid., 127–28.

15. Ibid., 128.

16. Elliott, *Conflict, Community, and Honor*, 16. Also Elliott, *1 Peter*, 128.

17. Horrell, "Product of a Petrine Circle?," 46–47.

18. Ibid., 48.

19. Ibid., 50.

20. Ibid., 51.

21. The sheer number of works attributed to Peter, including the two letters of Peter, a gospel, and an apocalypse, along with material describing him, most notably the Acts of Peter, in the first three centuries of the Jesus movement attests to Peter's significance as an authority who could be claimed for various rhetorical purposes.

22. Ibid., 54.

BIBLIOGRAPHY

Bartchy, S. Scott. "Divine Power, Community Formation and Leadership in the Acts of the Apostles." In *Community Formation in the Early Church and in the Church Today*, edited by Richard Longenecker, 89–104. Peabody, MA: Hendrickson, 2002.

Boissevain, Jeremy. *Friends of Friends: Networks, Manipulators, Coalitions*. Oxford: Basil Blackwell, 1974.

Cassidy, Richard J. *Four Times Peter: Portrayals of Peter in the Four Gospels and at Philippi*. Interfaces. Collegeville, MN: Liturgical Press, 2007.

Clottes, Jean, and David Lewis-Williams. *The Shamans of Prehistory: Trance and Magic in the Painted Caves*. Translated by Sophie Hawkes. New York: Harry N. Abrams, Inc., 1998.

Craffert, Pieter. "'I "Witnessed" the Raising of the Dead': Resurrection Accounts in Neuroanthropological Perspective." *Neotestamentica* 45, no. 1 (2011): 1–28.

———. "Shamanism and the Shamanic Complex." *Biblical Theology Bulletin* 41, no. 3 (2011): 151–61.

Crook, Zeba A. *Reconceptualising Conversion: Patronage, Loyalty, and Conversion in the Religions of the Ancient Mediterranean*. Beihefte zur Zeitschrift für die neutestamentliche Wissenschaft 130. Berlin: De Gruyter, 2004.

Ehrman, Bart D. *Peter, Paul and Mary Magdalene: The Followers of Jesus in History and Legend*. New York: Oxford University Press, 2006.

Elliott, John H. *Conflict, Community, and Honor: 1 Peter in Social-Scientific Perspective*. Cascade Companions. Eugene, OR: Cascade Books, 2007.

———. "Jesus the Israelite Was Neither a 'Jew' Nor a 'Christian': On Correcting Misleading Nomenclature." *Journal for the Study of the Historical Jesus* 5, no. 2 (2007): 119–54.

————. *1 Peter: A New Translation with Introduction and Commentary.* Anchor Bible 37B. New York: Doubleday, 2000.

————. *What Is Social-Scientific Criticism?* Guides to Biblical Scholarship. Minneapolis: Fortress, 1993.

Esler, Philip F. *Galatians.* New Testament Readings. London: Routledge, 1998.

Farthing, G. William. *The Psychology of Consciousness.* Englewood Cliffs, NJ: Prentice Hall, 1992.

Goodman, Felicitas D. *Ecstasy, Ritual, and Alternate Reality: Religion in a Pluralistic World.* Bloomington: Indiana University Press, 1988.

Hanson, K. C. "The Galilean Fishing Economy and the Jesus Tradition." *Biblical Theology Bulletin* 27 (1997): 99–111.

Hanson, K. C., and Douglas E. Oakman. *Palestine in the Time of Jesus: Social Structures and Social Conflicts.* 2nd ed. Minneapolis: Fortress, 2008.

Hansen, Marcus Lee. *The Problem of the Third-Generation Immigrant: A Reproduction of the 1937 Address with Introductions by Peter Kivisto and Oscar Handlin.* Rock Island, IL: Swenson Swedish Immigration Center, 1987.

Hellerman, Joseph H. *The Ancient Church as Family.* Minneapolis: Fortress, 2001.

Horrell, David G. "The Product of a Petrine Circle: A Reassessment of the Origin and Character of 1 Peter." *Journal for the Study of the New Testament* 86 (2002): 29–60.

Keener, Craig S. "The Pillars and the Right Hand of Fellowship in Galatians 2:9." *Journal of Greco-Roman Christianity and Judaism* 7 (2010): 51–58.

Kloppenborg, John S. *Excavating Q: The History and Setting of the Sayings Gospel.* Edinburgh: T & T Clark, 2000.

————. "*Exitus clari viri*: The Death of Jesus in Luke." *Toronto Journal of Theology* 8, no. 1 (1992): 106–20.

Malina, Bruce J. "From the Jesus Faction to the Synoptic Gospels." *Kontexte der Schrift: Band 2 Kultur, Politik, Religion, Sprache-Text: Wolfgang Stegemann zum 60. Geburtstag,* edited by Christian Strecker, 61–74. Stuttgart: Kohlhammer, 2005.

————. *The New Testament World: Insights from Cultural Anthropology.* 3rd ed. Louisville, KY: Westminster John Knox, 2001.

————. "Rhetorical Criticism and Social-Scientific Criticism: Why Won't Romanticism Leave Us Alone?" In *The Social World of the New*

Testament: Insights and Models, edited by Jerome H. Neyrey and Eric C. Stewart, 5–21. Peabody: Hendrickson, 2008.

———. *The Social Gospel of Jesus: The Kingdom of God in Mediterranean Perspective*. Minneapolis: Fortress, 2001.

———. *Timothy: Paul's Closest Associate*. Paul's Social Network: Brothers and Sisters in Faith. Collegeville, MN: Michael Glazier, 2008.

Malina, Bruce J., and Jerome H. Neyrey. *Portraits of Paul: An Archaeology of Ancient Personality*. Louisville, KY: Westminster John Knox, 1996.

Malina, Bruce J., and John J. Pilch. *Social-Science Commentary on the Book of Acts*. Minneapolis: Fortress, 2008.

———. *Social-Science Commentary on the Letters of Paul*. Minneapolis: Fortress, 2006.

Malina, Bruce J., and Richard L. Rohrbaugh. *Social-Science Commentary on the Gospel of John*. Minneapolis: Fortress, 1998.

———. *Social-Science Commentary on the Synoptic Gospels*. 2nd ed. Minneapolis: Fortress, 2003.

Meier, John P. *A Marginal Jew: Rethinking the Historical Jesus*. Volume 2: *Mentor, Message, and Miracles*. Anchor Bible Reference Library. New York: Doubleday, 1994.

———. *A Marginal Jew: Rethinking the Historical Jesus*. Volume 3: *Companions and Competitors*. Anchor Bible Reference Library. New York: Doubleday, 2001.

Neyrey, Jerome H. "The Social Location of Paul: Education as the Key." In *Fabrics of Discourse: Essays in Honor of Vernon K. Robbins*, edited by David B. Gowler, Gregory Bloomquist, and Duane F. Watson, 126–64. Harrisburg, PA: Trinity Press International, 2003.

Olick, Jeffrey K. "Collective Memory: The Two Cultures." *Sociological Theory* 17, no. 3 (1999): 333–48.

Olick, Jeffrey K., and Joyce Robbins, "Social Memory Studies: From 'Collective Memory' to the Sociology of Mnemonic Practices." *Annual Review of Anthropology* 24 (1998): 105–40.

Perkins, Pheme. *Peter: Apostle for the Whole Church*. Studies on Personalities of the New Testament. Columbia: University of South Carolina Press, 1994.

Pervo, Richard I. *Acts*. Hermeneia. Minneapolis: Fortress, 2009.

Pilch, John J. *Stephen: Paul and the Hellenist Israelites*. Paul's Social Network: Brothers and Sisters in Faith. Collegeville, MN: Michael Glazier, 2008.

————. *Visions and Healing in the Acts of the Apostles: How the Early Believers Experienced God.* Collegeville, MN: Liturgical Press, 2004.

Riley, Gregory J. *One Jesus, Many Christs: How Jesus Inspired Not One True Christianity, But Many; The Truth about Christian Origins.* San Francisco: HarperSanFrancisco, 1997.

Robinson, James M. *Jesus according to the Earliest Witnesses.* Minneapolis: Fortress, 2007.

Robinson, James M. et al., eds., *The Critical Edition of Q.* Hermeneia. Minneapolis: Fortress, 2000.

Rogers, Everett M. *Diffusion of Innovations.* 5th ed. New York: Free Press, 2003.

Rohrbaugh, Richard L. "Ethnocentrism and Historical Questions about Jesus." In *The Social Setting of Jesus and the Gospels*, 27–43. Minneapolis: Fortress, 2002.

————. "Honor: Core Value of the Biblical World." In *Understanding the Social World of the New Testament*, edited by Dietmar Neufeld and Richard E. DeMaris. London: Routledge, 2010.

Sanchez, David A. *From Patmos to the Barrio: Subverting Imperial Myths.* Minneapolis: Fortress, 2008.

Stendahl, Krister. "Paul and the Introspective Conscience of the West." *Harvard Theological Review* 56, no. 3 (1963): 199–215.

Sterling, Gregory. "*Mors philosophi*: The Death of Jesus in Luke." *Harvard Theological Review* 94, no. 4 (2001): 383–402.

Stewart, Eric C. *Gathered around Jesus: An Alternative Spatial Practice in the Gospel of Mark.* Matrix: The Bible in Mediterranean Context 6. Eugene, OR: Cascade, 2009.

————. "Social Stratification and Patronage in Ancient Mediterranean Societies." In *The New Testament in Cultural Context*, edited by Dietmar Neufeld and Richard E. DeMaris. London: Routledge, 2009.

Triandis, Harry C. *Individualism and Collectivism.* New Directions in Social Psychology. Boulder, CO: Westview, 1995.

Williams, Ritva H. "Social Memory and the Didachê." *Biblical Theology Bulletin* 36 (2006): 35–39.

————. *Stewards, Prophets, Keepers of the Word: Leadership in the Early Church.* Peabody, MA: Hendrickson, 2006.

de Young, Mary. "Moral Entrepreneur." In *The Blackwell Encyclopedia of Sociology*, ed. George Ritzer. Vol. 6. Malden, MA; Blackwell, 2007.

INDEX OF PERSONS AND SUBJECTS

SCRIPTURE INDEX

1:16-20	36		14:31	40
1:18	36		14:32-40	38
1:20	78n11		14:32-42	40
1:29-31	36		14:37	41
1:31	36		14:50	41
1:36-39	37, 45		14:54	41
2:4	36		14:66-72	40
3:13	37		14:68	41
3:13-19	37		14:69	41
3:16	37		14:71	41
3:19	36		14:72	41
4:10-20	37		16:7	41, 46, 49
5:35-43	37, 39			
6:6-11	40		*Luke*	
6:6-13	36, 37		4:1	58
6:13	48		4:14-30	58
6:45-52	45		4:16	62, 84n34
7:24-30	80n3		4:16-30	47
8:29	38, 39		4:18	58
8:31	38		4:21	58
8:32-33	48		4:31	47
8:33	38		4:38-39	47
8:34-38	39		4:38-41	47
9:2	39		4:42-43	37
9:2-8	39		5:3	47
9:5	39		6:13	47
9:31	38		6:27-28	85n10
9:32	38		7:1-10	80n3
9:33-37	39		7:7	65
10:23-27	39		8:49-56	48, 60
10:28	37, 39		8:54	60
10:30	40		9:1	48
10:32	38		9:2	48
10:33-34	38		9:20	48
10:35-40	39		9:21-22	48, 58
10:41-50	39		9:28-37	48
11:21	40		9:29	48
11:24	40		9:31	48
13:3-4	40		9:32	48
13:5-31	40		9:33	48, 49
13:32	40		9:36	49
14:27	40		9:44-45	58
14:30	40		10:5-9	81n11